"A moving, searching book in which psychoanalysis and spirituality nourish, add to and enrich one another as complex, multidimensional realities continue to grow. Through interaction of overlapping experiential practices, possibilities of the human find new life. My congratulations to Gideon Lev for undertaking the task of doing each domain justice, while bringing out the power of their communion in clinical practice and appreciative reflection."

Michael Eigen *PhD, author of* The Psychoanalytic Mystic, Faith, *and* Kabbalah and Psychoanalysis

"Lev's book is both modest and extremely ambitious. He recognises that there has been a 'spiritual turn' in psychoanalytic therapy. He didn't invent spiritually sensitive psychoanalysis. But his achievement is to demonstrate a deep understanding that there remains a pressing need to mainstream this turn so that it ceases to be niche, or remain the property of 'transpersonal' or 'Jungian' therapies. The original way in which the book is structured achieves this important and timely goal. Of equal significance is the broad range of spiritual and religious traditions upon which Lev draws. This represents a necessary ecumenicalism. At a time when the fastest growing approach to spirituality is termed SBNR (spiritual but not religious), it is the moment for psychoanalysis to make a somewhat different contribution than it has up to now. Maybe spiritually sensitive psychoanalysis is a new tradition within which spirit coils weaves its web? And maybe this book will find its way onto all relevant reading lists?"

Andrew Samuels *PhD, author of* Persons, Passions, Psychotherapy, Politics *and* A New Anatomy of Spirituality

Spiritually Sensitive Psychoanalysis

This book provides an accessible introduction to spiritually sensitive psychoanalysis, an analytic tradition characterized by sensitivity to the spiritual and religious dimensions of human life and oriented towards spiritual growth.

Psychoanalysis has historically evinced severe suspicion to all ideas and ideals of religion and spirit. However, in recent years, a new analytic approach is emerging, which recognizes faith and spirituality as crucial parts of full, satisfying psychic life. This book explores the unique ways in which this approach refers to and understands core analytic issues such as transference, interpretation, psychopathology and psychic development. It goes on to expound the approach's understanding of the analytic relationship and the way it influences the spiritual person. It also discusses the tensions arising between this emerging school of thought and the existing body of psychoanalytic knowledge.

Psychoanalysis is a practice that deals with the most profound questions of life and creates shifts in the way reality is perceived. Discussing freely and deeply its spiritual aspects and aspirations will enlighten analysts new to the emerging spiritually sensitive tradition, as well as those who are more familiar with it, and who are looking for a comprehensive description of this fresh approach to analysis.

Gideon Lev, PhD, is a clinical psychologist, philosopher and spiritual seeker. He teaches at Tel Aviv University and is a staff writer for the Israeli newspaper *Haaretz*. His previous books are *Ilove* (2015) and *Truth Love Faith: A Psychoanalytic and Historic Look at the Meaning of Life* (2018).

Routledge Introductions to Contemporary Psychoanalysis
Aner Govrin, Ph.D.
Series Editor
Tair Caspi, Ph.D.
Executive Editor
Yael Peri Herzovich
Assistant Editor

"Routledge Introductions to Contemporary Psychoanalysis" is one of the prominent psychoanalytic publishing ventures of our day. It will comprise dozens of books that will serve as concise introductions dedicated to influential concepts, theories, leading figures and techniques in psychoanalysis covering every important aspect of psychoanalysis.

The length of each book is fixed at 40,000 words.

The series' books are designed to be easily accessible to provide informative answers in various areas of psychoanalytic thought. Each book will provide updated ideas on topics relevant to contemporary psychoanalysis – from the unconscious and dreams, projective identification and eating disorders, through neuropsychoanalysis, colonialism and spiritually sensitive psychoanalysis. Books will also be dedicated to prominent figures in the field, such as Melanie Klein, Jaque Lacan, Sandor Ferenczi, Otto Kernberg and Michael Eigen.

Not serving solely as an introduction for beginners, the purpose of the series is to offer compendiums of information on particular topics within different psychoanalytic schools. We ask authors to not only review a topic but also address the readers with their own personal views and contribution to the specific chosen field. Books will make intricate ideas comprehensible without compromising their complexity.

We aim to make contemporary psychoanalysis more accessible to both clinicians and the general educated public.

Aner Govrin – Editor

Psychoanalytic Field Theory: A Contemporary Introduction
Giuseppe Civitarese

Psychoanalysis and Colonialism: A Contemporary Introduction
Sally Swartz

W.R. Bion's Theories of Mind: A Contemporary Introduction
Annie Reiner

Herbert Rosenfeld: A Contemporary Introduction
Robert Hinshelwood

Neuropsychoanalysis: A Contemporary Introduction
Georg Northoff

Spiritually Sensitive Psychoanalysis: A Contemporary Introduction
Gideon Lev

Psychoanalysis and Homosexuality: A Contemporary Introduction
Leezah Hertzmann and Juliet Newbigin

Melanie Klein: A Contemporary Introduction
Penelope Garvey

Spiritually Sensitive Psychoanalysis

A Contemporary Introduction

Gideon Lev

LONDON AND NEW YORK

Designed cover image: © Michal Heiman, Asylum 1855-2020, The Sleeper (video, psychoanalytic sofa and Plate 34), exhibition view, Herzliya Museum of Contemporary Art, 2017

First published 2023
by Routledge
4 Park Square, Milton Park, Abingdon, Oxon OX14 4RN

and by Routledge
605 Third Avenue, New York, NY 10158

Routledge is an imprint of the Taylor & Francis Group, an informa business

© 2023 Gideon Lev

The right of Gideon Lev to be identified as author of this work has been asserted in accordance with sections 77 and 78 of the Copyright, Designs and Patents Act 1988.

All rights reserved. No part of this book may be reprinted or reproduced or utilised in any form or by any electronic, mechanical, or other means, now known or hereafter invented, including photocopying and recording, or in any information storage or retrieval system, without permission in writing from the publishers.

Trademark notice: Product or corporate names may be trademarks or registered trademarks, and are used only for identification and explanation without intent to infringe.

British Library Cataloguing-in-Publication Data
A catalogue record for this book is available from the British Library

ISBN: 978-0-367-54865-0 (hbk)
ISBN: 978-0-367-54866-7 (pbk)
ISBN: 978-1-003-09093-9 (ebk)

DOI: 10.4324/9781003090939

Typeset in Times New Roman
by KnowledgeWorks Global Ltd.

Contents

Acknowledgements xi

Introduction: A breath of life 1

PART I
Spirituality in context 11

1 Things in heaven and earth: Psychoanalysis and spirit 13

2 A very peculiar science: A brief cultural history of psychoanalysis 24

PART II
A spiritual model 41

3 Religious instinct, sacred unconscious and the area of faith: Towards a new model of the psyche 43

4 God-representations, mystical addictions
   and spiritual bypasses: Adaptive
   treatment goals   57

5 Morality, selflessness, transcendence:
   Transformative treatment goals   61

PART III
Essential spirituality   **75**

6 The window is the absence of the wall:
   Psychoanalysis as a spiritual practice   77

7 A love through cure: The spirit of
   analytic relationship   91

   Conclusion: Ecstasy and suffering resting
   in one another: The contribution of
   spiritually sensitive psychoanalysis   111

   References   124
   Index   146

Acknowledgements

I would like to thank Aner Govrin, editor of the Routledge Contemporary Introductions book series, for inviting me to write this book. Govrin's profound knowledge and generous presence have served a crucial part in the formation of my thoughts, and I am grateful for them.

Orit Sen-Gupta has accompanied me for many years on my path of development from a young student and meditation practitioner to a qualified psychologist. Her encouragement has allowed me to find the courage to implement spiritual elements in my work with patients.

Michal Alperstein, my beloved life partner, has supported me throughout the writing of this book, giving advice, reading my work and patiently bearing with the difficulties that such a project entails. Her loving presence in my life is the main reason I manage to write, work, practice and keep developing, by myself, with my patients and with her. I am deeply thankful.

I have drawn material from some of my early papers for this book and wish to thank my publishers for granting permission to use this material here. "Morality, selflessness, transcendence: On treatment goals of a spiritually sensitive psychoanalysis" (2015) was published by William Alanson White Institute of Psychiatry, Psychoanalysis & Psychology and the William Alanson White Psychoanalytic

Society in *Contemporary Psychoanalysis*, *51*(3), 523–556. "The question of analytic aims: Psychoanalysis and the changing formulations of the life worth living" (2016) was published by the American Psychological Association in *Psychoanalytic Psychology*, *33*(2), 312–333. "Getting to the heart of life: Psychoanalysis as a spiritual practice" (2017) was published by William Alanson White Institute of Psychiatry, Psychoanalysis & Psychology and the William Alanson White Psychoanalytic Society in *Contemporary Psychoanalysis*, *53*(2), 222–246. "Poetics of reconcilement: Psychoanalysis and dilemmas of faith" (2018) was published by the American Psychological Association in *Psychoanalytic Psychology*, *35*(1), 38–45.

Introduction
A breath of life

For about a century, psychoanalysis was suspicious of any kind of religious or spiritual ideas. Freud (1930; 1927) held that religion was a mass delusion and a form of wish fulfilment. He even ruled out in advance any question regarding the meaning and value of life since "objectively neither has any existence" (1937, p. 436).

Consequently, psychoanalysts tended to be hostile, or at least indifferent towards spiritual issues. Sorenson (2004a) searched the Library of Congress for publications about psychoanalysis and spirituality and did not find a single volume in the three decades between 1950 and 1979. In the next decade he found one.

Since then, though, the picture has rapidly changed. In the first two decades of the 21st century, one can easily notice a dramatic increase in the number of analysts demonstrating a burgeoning interest in the positive potential of spiritual experiences.

From this new perspective, religion, faith and spirituality are seen not necessarily as evidence of pathology, or as attempts to escape reality, as Freud and his followers interpreted them, but as expressions of a kind of achievement – emotional, moral and cultural – that could be expected to emerge through a successful analytic process (Blass, 2004). They are thus considered important parts of

DOI: 10.4324/9781003090939-1

full, satisfying psychic life. More and more papers, conferences and even series of books such as Routledge's new *Psyche and Soul* attest to this shift. Unprecedentedly, psychoanalytic journals devoted whole issues to a generally positive discussion of religion and spirituality.[1] Something strange happened to psychoanalysis, wrote Arnowitz (2010): it seems to have "(re)found religion" (p. 71).[2]

Psychoanalysis becoming "sensitive" to the spiritual is arguably one of the biggest changes the discipline has gone through since its inception. Some have said this is as dramatic and far-reaching "paradigm shift" for psychoanalysis as was the Copernican revolution for 16th-century astronomy (Sorenson, 2004a). A tradition which was hostile to anything to do with spirit and religion has become, as I will show in this book, highly involved in these matters, to the point it can be considered to be a spiritual practice or discipline in itself (Lev, 2017; Marcus, 2021).

Following this paradigm shift, analysts today do not hesitate delving into each and every aspect and branch of religious, spiritual or mystical occupation. They investigate Islam (e.g. Akhtar, 2008; El Shakry, 2017; Pandolfo, 2018); Buddhism and Zen Buddhism (Safran, 2003; Molino, 2014; Bobrow, 2020); Hinduism (Akhtar, 2005; Cunningham, 2006); Judaism and Kabbalah (Starr, 2008; Eigen, 2012); Christianity (Hoffman, 2010; 2020; Bland & Strawn, 2014); Confucianism, Taoism and Stoic philosophy (Marcus, 2003; Silverberg, 2011); mysticism (Sayers, 2003; Parsons, 2013); Gnosticism (Gordon, 2004) and traditional religion and perceptions of Divinity (Jones, 2007; Spero, 2008). They even write about parapsychology and about magic (Mayer, 2007; Brottman, 2009; Rosenbaum, 2011). This is a *very* limited sample.

Despite the wide range of publications on psychoanalysis and various aspects of spirituality, the trend as a whole has not been adequately addressed in psychoanalytic literature so far. Hence, what it actually means to be "spiritually sensitive" has not been comprehensively discussed. Analysts have adopted a favourable view of spirituality, but never defined and described in detail what is a spiritually sensitive psychoanalysis – what does it contribute to psychoanalysis and how is its practice different from exiting approaches. This new, consolidating analytic tradition still has no single volume that summarizes the various ideas encompassed within it. This book is thus an attempt to fill this gap and to make the term "spiritually sensitive" a little clearer. It presents and summarizes for the first time the budding theories of development, transference and psychopathology as they are newly understood by spiritually sensitive psychoanalysis, as well as the unique ways this new therapeutic school understands the analytic relationship and sets its therapeutic goals.

Before doing that, an attempt will be made to clarify the complex concept that is at the centre of this book. "Spirituality," which derives from the Latin *spiritus*, meaning "breath of life," was described as the ongoing transformation which occurs when one is involved in some sort of relationality with what can be described as transcendental or "unconditional" (Waaijman, 1993, p. 45).

Elkins (1988) tried to give a phenomenological description of "the spiritual," and checked what people actually mean when they use the word. He offered the following definition: "Spirituality ... is a way of being and experiencing that comes through awareness of a transcendent dimension and that is characterized by certain identifiable values in regard to self, others, nature, life, and whatever one considers to be the Ultimate" (quoted in West, 2000, p. 8).

These descriptions might sound somewhat vague and general. Indeed, one of the characteristics of contemporary spirituality, which makes it difficult to define precisely, is that it has no leader – no Moses, Siddhartha, Jesus or Muhammad. This is perhaps the first major religious system in history to have evolved in this way, from the masses and not from a leader or prophet (Forman, 2004). That is why it also has no set of rules of conduct and belief.

Spirituality is not based on specific values and rituals, as was the case with all religious movements to date, but a collection of practices whose boundaries are particularly permeable and which include complex and sometimes inconsistent beliefs and approaches. Samuels (2001) beautifully described this variety:

> Spirituality may be rooted in traditional, formal religion. Or it may be a highly idiosyncratic and personal affair. Or both. Spirituality may be located above us, at ground level (even in the body) or below, in an underworld. Or on all three levels. Spirituality may be understood as universal, comprehensive and catholic with a small 'c'. Or it may be experienced and expressed radically differently according to time, place, age, sex, sexual orientation, ethnicity, class and one's physical and psychological health. Or both. Spirituality may be regarded as beyond the transpersonal, transcending the human realms of existence. Or it may exist only in a relational, intersubjective, interactional setting. Or both. Spirituality may be seen as a substance or essence – breath, pneuma, ruach. Or it may be more of a perspective on experience. Or both.
> (p. 122)

A variety of currents, opinions, ideals, beliefs and thoughts is thus included within the broad title of "spirituality." These perceptions touch all planes of existence and are expressed in interpersonal relationships, in patterns of consumption and recreation, in the education system, in the health system and even in the business world (Forman, 2004; Heelas, 2008).

Being such a general concept, "spirituality" is difficult to define – as is "game," for example (Wittgenstein, 1953).

However, just as games can be identified despite the huge differences between chess and ping-pong, for instance, due to some "family resemblance," so spirituality has a core that can be identified within its range of expressions. Heelas (1996) elaborated on the differences between various spiritual streams, only to conclude that beneath the heterogeneity one can find a remarkable consistency. Forman (2004) wrote that although members of the spiritual movement today come from all religions around the world, and even though they have different perspectives, vocabularies and traditions, they share a deep and detailed world-view.

At the root of this world-view are two central, interrelated principles around which the multitude of practices, traditions and beliefs of the innumerable spiritual currents are organized. The first, "ontological principle," speaks of the existence of an Absolute. This Absolute is beyond the myriad phenomena that humans face in the material world, yet it is not separated or detached from these phenomena. This principle leads to a holistic conception of reality according to which all things in the universe are interconnected (Woodhouse, 1996). This view is dramatically different from the common modern and postmodern conception of the universe as mechanical, as it sees the universe as a unity that is intelligent, self-organized and ever-evolving (DiCarlo, 1996). The whole of nature is perceived as imbued with a consciousness or life-force (Herrick, 2003). This is basically a "panentheistic" world view, according to which all things are in the ultimate, that is, all things are made up of a single principle, but that one principle is not limited to those worldly phenomena (Forman, 2004).[3]

Holism and panentheism are linked to the "Perennial Philosophy," according to which the world and our life, as they are perceived through our senses and through science, are only the outer shell of an invisible, inner and causal reality. The term "Perennial Philosophy" was coined by 17th-century philosopher Gottfried Wilhelm Leibniz and was revived in the 20th century by Aldous Huxley (1946), who defined it as "The metaphysic that recognizes a divine Reality substantial to the world of things and lives and minds" (p. 1).[4]

The second, "epistemological principle," which underlies the spiritual movement, is linked to the psychology of Perennial Philosophy. As Huxley (1946) described it, this psychology finds in the psyche or soul something similar to, or even identical with, divine reality.

The belief is hence that human consciousness has almost unlimited growth potential, as it is part of the panentheistic Absolute (Herrick, 2003). The profound goal of those who espouse the spiritual world-view is to recognize and affirm that holistic unity, to connect personally, through the self and beyond it, to the essence behind all things, of which the self is also an expression. It is thus "[an] ethic that places man's final end in the knowledge of the immanent and transcendent Ground of all being" (Huxley, 1946, p. 1).[5]

The assumptions and goals of the spiritual movement can be summarized as follows: the whole world is an expression of a more comprehensive divine nature. Within every person is hidden a higher divine self that is an expression of the same divine nature; This nature can be aroused and can become the centre of a person's life – and this is the reason for the existence of each individual person (Heelas, 1996). As Michael Lerner, editor of the spiritual journal *Tikkun*, put it: "At heart, our deepest desire is to realize our oneness with that power, that transcendent reality that is both within us, at the core of our being, and all around us, saturating every part of this sacred universe" (quoted in Forman, 2004, p. 61).

This desire is perhaps universal, and not held only by self-declared "spiritual" people. Eminent philosopher

Charles Taylor (2007) argued all humans have a sense of "fullness" – which is *always* "a reflection of transcendent reality" (p. 769). This is why, he continued, if we settle with the immanent – only the material, or even only the psychological – this fullness is hard to realize.

Taylor is part of a long tradition of philosophers, starting with Plato or even earlier, to have argued as much. Today, remarkably, many psychoanalysts seem to agree. In a successful analysis a variety of psychic changes are achieved, wrote Ulanov (2000), but *the most important one* is concerned with what the patient perceives as relating to "some transcendent meaning and purpose" (p. 41).

A completely new stream of analytic thinking has evolved around this view. This book is dedicated to introducing how it sees core analytic issues such as transference, interpretation, psychopathology and psychic development, the way it understands psychic health and the life worth living and how these understandings affect its therapeutic goals.

The book is divided into three parts. The first part puts the emergence of this new analytic school in historical context. Chapter 1 offers an original and comprehensive review of the history of psychoanalytic attitudes towards various modes of faith. It begins with a systematic examination of Freud's approach, demonstrating that contrary to the common understanding of his attitude as one-sided, radical atheism, Freud displayed ambivalence on this issue. After his death, it will be shown, psychoanalysis as a discipline have effected a split: while the psychoanalytic establishment adopted and reinforced the anti-religious stance, a small number of prominent analytic thinkers nurtured the possibility of integrating faith into their practice. Following that, Chapter 2 presents the cultural and historical background to the emergence of spiritually sensitive psychoanalysis. It demonstrates how, in the last decades of the previous century, Western culture went through a shift from a scientific-positivistic world-view to a post-modern one, a shift which allowed a parallel shift in psychoanalysis from Classical to Relational modes. In the 21st-century culture, it is then shown, a spiritual world-view gained ascendancy, and this paved the way to the emergence of a corresponding analytic mode.

The second part goes into the details of this analytic mode. Chapter 3 describes some of the new ideas presented by spiritually sensitive analysts, in regard to basic analytic concepts such as transference and countertransference, the unconscious, instincts, pathology and technique. Chapters 4 and 5 proceed to expound on the central issue of treatment goals, which distinguish spiritually sensitive psychoanalysis from other modes of analysis. Chapter 4 describes "adaptive" spiritual goals, which aim at reducing and healing pathological patterns of spirituality, while Chapter 5 describes "transformative" spiritual goals which aim at deepening the patient's spiritual experience, for example by developing a moral stance of compassion and responsibility or by lessening preoccupation with the self.

The third part discusses spiritual elements inherent in the psychoanalytic procedure, regardless of the analysts' or analysands' interest in spirituality. Chapter 6 shows that while psychoanalysis is commonly considered a treatment method, a procedure for investigating the mind and a general theory of mind, it also satisfies criteria for being a spiritual practice in and of itself. Chapter 7 discusses love, which has always been *the* supreme virtue of spiritual traditions, and shows how the analytic encounter's setting is uniquely shaped to encourage and allow a high form of love.

Finally, in the Conclusion, spiritually sensitive psychoanalysis' special contribution to the spiritual person will be discussed, by comparing it with the workings of spiritual traditions and of other spiritually sensitive psychologies. I will point to the unique aspects of this new mode of therapy, and how these offer to embrace and enhance our psyche and soul.

Notes

1. *International Journal of Applied Psychoanalytic Studies*, volume 1(1); *Psychoanalytic Inquiry*, volume 28(5) and volume 40(5); *Journal of the American Academy of Psychoanalysis and Dynamic Psychiatry*, volume 37(1).
2. A similar trend can be discerned in psychiatry (e.g., Huguelet & Koenig, 2009) and in psychodynamic psychotherapy, evidenced by the founding of the APA's journal *Spirituality in Clinical Practice*, starting 2014, and publications such as Pargament (2007).
3. 'Panentheism' comes from the combination of the Latin words, "pan," "en" and "theos" and means literally "all in deity."
4. Albert Einstein can perhaps serve as an example of this stance. The great scientist said that although he considers himself an atheist, he is a religious person and added that for him what constitutes "true religiosity" is the knowledge and the emotion that "what is impenetrable to us really exists, manifesting itself as the highest wisdom and the most radiant beauty which our dull faculties can comprehend only in their most primitive forms" (quoted in Fadiman, 1990, p. 6).
5. Between the first principle, which speaks of an Absolute *beyond* the myriad of phenomena in the world, and the second, which emphasizes the existence of that Absolute *within* the world (and specifically, in human inwardness), there is a tension that is essential to spirituality. Kovel (1985) wrote beautifully about this:

The spiritual attitude oscillates back and forth, now locating spirit beyond the given world (that is, transcendently), now recognizing spirit in objects at hand (that is, immanently). In truth, spirit is neither and both: in and out of what is given to us at the same time. The problem for spirituality is to comprehend this difficult truth without going mad or yielding to domination.

(quoted in Simmonds, 2004, p. 957)

Part I

Spirituality in context

Chapter 1

Things in heaven and earth

Psychoanalysis and spirit

Freud offered in his diverse writings a criticism of the religious worldview that accumulated to one of the severest attacks it has ever faced. Already in *The Psychopathology of Everyday Life*, Freud (1901) wrote that the mythic perception of the world, which deeply pervaded all religions, "is nothing but psychology projected into the external world" (p. 258).

From here arose his basic assumption, according to which religion is to be understood not as a description of reality, but as a consequence of a human psycho-cognitive activity. The mistake of believers, who assume that religion describes an objective state of affairs, thus ascribes religion to the category of "mass-delusions" (1930, p. 81). In fact, Freud (1927) claimed that religious ideas are nothing more than a way of coping with the terror of existence and the transitoriness of human life, an expression of "the oldest, strongest and most urgent wishes of mankind" – for a benevolent rule of a divine Providence; the establishment of a moral world-order; and the prolongation of earthly existence in a future life (p. 30). The ritualistic religious preoccupation was compared by Freud (1907) to an obsessional neurosis.

In Freud's depth analysis of religious faith, he found its origin, like anything else's, in early childhood.[1] The period

DOI: 10.4324/9781003090939-3

in which the human infant is completely dependent for its existence on the care of the parents is especially prolonged and leaves a deep mark on the psyche. In adulthood, when the person again perceives how truly forlorn and weak he is when confronted with the great forces of life, "he feels his condition as he did in childhood, and attempts to deny his own despondency by a regressive revival of the forces which protected his infancy" (1910, p. 123).

The forces which protected the infant were his parents, therefor their image, and especially the image of the strong father creates the mould for the image of god. When a man understands that his helplessness lasts throughout life, he becomes attached to the existence of a father, "but this time a more powerful one" (1927, p. 30).

Another explanation Freud (1918) gave to the tenacity of religion is a social one. Religion is included in the education of children in all cultures, as it puts a restraint on their sexual impulses and lowers the importance of the person's family relationships in comparison to the larger community. In this way, religion allows the "untamed and fear-ridden" child to become "social, well-behaved, and amenable to education" (p. 115).

Responding to Freud's criticism, his old friend, the philosopher, mystic and Nobel laureate writer Romain Rolland, argued that the origin of religious energy does not lie in a belief in a personal god or other comforting and calming ideas – but in a unique state of consciousness, a subjective sensation of some absolute or of eternity. Freud didn't withdraw his claim and in *Civilization and its Discontents* (1930) argued that the sensation described by Rolland, termed by Freud "oceanic feeling," does not point to a transcendent entity but stems from very early sensations the baby feels towards the universe and which are later connected to religion.

To conclude, in Freud's (1930) words, the whole subject of religion (and especially the belief in a personal God) is "so patently infantile, so foreign to reality, that to anyone with a friendly attitude to humanity it is painful to think that the great majority of mortals will never be able to rise above this view of life" (p. 74).[2]

Perceiving faith as illusion, understanding the deep religious experience as regression and reducing God to a displacement of the father's image became the cornerstones of psychoanalysis' relation to the religious experience and *weltanschauung*. But delving deeper into the Freudian cannon reveals that here too his thought was highly complex.

In the essay in which Freud undermined the oceanic feeling appears one of his most mystery-laden utterances relating to the object of religious faith. Freud seems to have opened here a wicket to the possibility of an existence of something beyond illusion, neurosis or regression: "The origin of the religious attitude can be traced back in clear outlines as far as the feeling of infantile helplessness. *There may be something further behind that*, but for the present it is wrapped in obscurity" (Freud, 1930, p. 72; emphasis mine).

In the corpus of his writings, Freud referred again and again to the soul (*die Seele*) of man as the object of his research, seeing psychoanalysis as "part of psychology which is dedicated to the science of the soul" (Bettelheim, 1982, p. 75). He even declared (1926) that the title "secular pastoral worker" describes well the analyst's function and in the 31st lecture of the *New Introductory Lectures* he (1933a) compared psychoanalysis' therapeutic efforts with mystical practices. Freud even wrote favourably about the possibility of telepathy (1921 [1941]; 1922), and in a 1921 letter to the well-known supernatural phenomena researcher Hereward Carrington, Freud confessed: "If I had my life to live over again I should devote myself to psychical research rather that to psychoanalysis" (quoted in Jones, 1957, p. 419).

Ernst Jones told that in the years prior to World War I, he had several conversations with Freud regarding occultism and other similar topics. Freud was extremely fond of entertaining his listener, particularly after midnight, with descriptions of strange or uncanny experiences with patients, characteristically about misfortunes or deaths. "He had a particular relish for such stories and was evidently impressed by their more mysterious aspects," reported Jones (1957, p. 408). A sworn rationalist himself, Jones protested against the more bizarre stories, and Freud used to reply with his *favourite quotation* (a fact not to be taken lightly in itself): "There are more things in heaven and earth than are dreamt of in your philosophy." In instances when Freud's stories were concerned with clairvoyant visions of episodes at a distance, or visitations from departed spirits, Jones insisted on his criticism. Freud responded, according to his biographer, by saying "I don't like it at all myself, but there is some truth in it" – and thus, wrote Jones, "both sides of his nature [came into] expression in a short sentence" (ibid).

In one of those nightly meetings, Jones again expressed his doubts and wondered how far could such beliefs be extended – if one could believe in mental processes floating in the air (telepathy), one could go on to a belief in angels. Freud closed the discussion at this point (it was about 3 am) with the remark: "Quite so, even der liebe Gott" (quite so, and even in the good God). The words were said in a jocular tone, Jones (1957) remarked, but there was "something searching also in the glance, and I went away not entirely happy lest there be some more serious undertone as well" (p. 408).

Indeed, Freud wrote he saw religion as a highly respected institution, whose importance does not fall from that of the scientific project. In his lecture about worldviews, Freud (1933b) wondered why doesn't religion put an end to the "hopeless" dispute between religious emotion and scientific logic with the following sympathetic declaration which he wanted to put in religion's mouth:

> It is a fact that I cannot give you what is commonly called 'truth'; if you want that, you must keep to science. But what I have to offer you is something incomparably more beautiful, more consoling and more uplifting than anything you could get from science. And because of that, I say to you that it is true in another, higher sense.
>
> (p. 172)

Ludwig Binswanger, one of the pioneers of existential psychology and a long-time correspondent of Freud, recounted a conversation the two held in Semmering in 1927. After discussing a case, Binswanger suggested that the reason some patients were unable to take the decisive step towards psychoanalytic insight had to do with an inability to engage in a type of "spiritual communication" with the physician. Binswanger wrote: "I could scarcely believe my ears when I heard him say, 'Yes, the spirit is everything'" (1957, p. 81). Binswanger continued: "I was inclined to surmise that by 'spirit' he meant, in this case something like intelligence. But then Freud continued: 'Humankind has always known that it possesses spirit; I had to show it that there are also instincts'" (p. 81). Freud's strategy succeeded, perhaps, too well.

Reminding humanity it possesses also "spirit," and not only instincts, might be one of spiritually sensitive psychoanalysis' current missions, to which Freud perhaps pointed prophetically nearing the end of his life. In his postscript to *An Autobiographical Study*, Freud mentioned his negative valuation of religion in works such as *The Future of an Illusion*. Later in life, so he wrote in this last addition to his account of his life, he found a formula that "did better justice to it ... [by] granting that its power lies in the *truth* which it contains" (1935, p. 72).

Freud's relation to faith in what lies beyond the logical and immanent was, as shown, complex and not unequivocal. There is no doubt he was, after all, an atheist, but he contained in him also other attractions. It seems it can be stated he did not want to turn his life's work, psychoanalysis, into an icon of anti-religiosity. To his long-time companion, the priest and analyst Oskar Pfister, Freud (1963) wrote in 1930: "Let us be quite clear on the point that the views expressed in my book [*The Future of an Illusion*] form no part of analytic theory" (p. 117).

But hostility towards anything to do with faith did become eventually an integral part of analytic theory, leading to religion and spirituality receiving over the years problematic treatment from analysis as have few other expressions of cultural diversity, including socioeconomic status, race, ethnicity, gender, or sexual orientation (Sorenson, 2004a).

A typical example of this hostile attitude can be found with Deutch, who described an analysis of a Catholic teacher. The patient felt by the end of analysis "completely satisfied," and yet the analysis was evaluated by Deutch as incomplete since the patient didn't decide to leave the convent she was connected with (Deutch, 1932, quoted in Sorenson, 2004a, pp. 153–154). Similarly, Fenichel (1939) proudly wrote how, as his patients progressed in their analyses, their "attachment to religion has ended" (p. 316). Black (2006) mentioned that expressing religious faith was considered by analysts equivalent to exhibiting neuroticism in public, noting how Melanie Klein, who was proud in her rejection of religion, stressed late at life her wish that her funeral be devoid of any religious characteristics.

The rejecting attitude did not stop short at expressions of institutionalized religion. Buddhism, for example, which holds no view of a creator god, did not escape the analytic whip. In one of the first psychoanalytic references to the Eastern doctrine, Alexander (1931) described Buddhist practice as "a sort of artificial schizophrenia" (p. 130) and as "a narcissistic-masochistic affair" (p. 131). Seventy years later, in 1994, senior analysts, who were involved in Buddhist practice, refused to participate in a conference titled *The Suffering Self: A Dialogue between Psychoanalysts and Buddhists* for fear of harming their reputation (Roland, 2003).

Until the end of the 20th century, the anti-religious stance remained the common attitude in psychoanalysis (with few exceptions which will be described shortly). It was even termed "the received view" (Parsons, 2007, p. 87). LaMothe, Arnold and Crane (1998) found that only in about 1% of case descriptions presented in major psychoanalytic journals in the 1990s there was any attempt to explore and integrate religious experience in the patient's therapy. Simmonds (2004) compared the way psychoanalysis treated religious faith to the way it used to treat femininity. Historically, she wrote, psychoanalysis regarded women as inferior and less developed. Similarly, Simmonds claimed, psychoanalysis finds it difficult to deal with spirituality without prejudice.

This attitude of the psychoanalytic establishment towards anything which smelled like spirit can be understood also as part of the attempt to medicalize the profession. Especially in the United States, Ego psychologists tried to make psychoanalysis into a completely scientific, medical endeavour, and as such were inherently opposed to religion, as we will see in more detail in the next chapter.

In contrast to the "medicalizing," positivist, antitheistic trend, arose in the second half of 20th century some psychoanalytic attempts to treat faith in a more open and curious way. These were indeed very few and remained outside the centre of discussion, but it is interesting to note they often came from prominent and influential thinkers. One might say that psychoanalysis as a discipline performed a sort of a "split" (Lev, 2018): While the psychoanalytic mainstream fully adopted, and even strengthened Freud's declared atheist stance, some of the more original psychoanalytic thinkers took on themselves guarding that spark of interest in the transcendent that flickered in the discipline's founder's *Seele*, and which he exposed mostly in private communications.

Those thinkers introduced ideas quite different from "the received view." In the United States, such ideas were offered by Erik Erikson, especially in his favourable biographies of religious leaders Luther (1958) and Gandhi (1969), and Erich Fromm, who was the first to write about psychoanalysis and Zen Buddhism, and even claimed that the analytic method of exposing the unconscious, if carried to its ultimate consequences, "may be a step toward enlightenment" (1960, p. 79). Fromm (1966) also introduced the "x experience," which was his psychoanalytic formulation to describe experiences of transcendence. Heinz Kohut (1966) offered the idea of "cosmic narcissism," which involved a possible, though difficult to attain shift of the narcissistic cathexes "from the self to a concept of participation in a supraindividual and timeless existence" (p. 266). And Hans Loewald (1978) claimed the religious experience was repressed in the society of his days even more than sexuality, which made its release, and not abolition, a worthy analytic aim.

Across the ocean, other attempts were made to connect psychoanalysis with the life of faith and spirit. In France, Lacan offered the mystically laden concepts of "jouissance" and "the Real." Deeply influenced by Plotinus, Lacan even thought his work should be considered "of the same order" as mysticism (1982; quoted in Parsons, 2007, p. 91). In England, Fairbairn introduced into psychoanalytic theory strains of the Calvinist narrative according to which God created humans in His image, capable of love and desire, first towards Him and then towards each other, thus making us beings who are relational by their very nature (Hoffman, 2004). Balint (1968) disproved Freud's concept of primary narcissism, on which his oceanic experience theory depended, replacing it with a theory of "primary love." Balint (1968) claimed that "unio mystica" – the re-establishment of the harmonious interpenetrating mix-up between the individual and the most important parts of his environment, his love objects – is the "ultimate aim" of all humanity (p. 74). Also in England, Milner (1973) presented an appreciative approach to mysticism, while Gunthrip and Rycroft tried to bridge the gap between psychoanalysis and faith (see Gordon, 2004). And Winnicott (1965) wrote about the "incommunicado" element which he saw as the core of personality, beyond id, ego and superego, and which he described as "sacred" (p. 187).

The most elaborated early spiritual psychoanalytic position is probably the one presented by Bion (1970). In sharp contrast with the common psychoanalytic discourse, he suggested that what allows therapeutic change is more to do with transformations in F (faith) in O ("ultimate reality" or "absolute truth") than with broadening of K (knowledge).

Yet despite the work of these influential thinkers, the attitude in psychoanalytic institutes towards faith, religion and spirituality remained hostile or at most indifferent. In an autobiographical account of her professional life, Flynn Campbell (2005) wrote that during her many years of psychoanalytic training, she can recall no case presentation that included a description of a patient's spiritual life: "We discussed their sex lives, their salaries, their most personal fantasies, and yet their spirituality never came up; or if it did, it was only in blatantly pathological cases" (p. 62).

Faith and religion were thus projected outside of mainstream psychoanalytic research and practice, mainly into the domain of Jung's analytical psychology. In many ways, this is not surprising. The most dramatic schism in the history of the psychoanalytic movement, the one between Freud and the person he initially called "my *successor* and crown prince" (Freud, 1909, p. 218), was in large part a result of contrasting perceptions of faith and religion (Palmer, 1997).

Following this split, Freud fortified the anti-religious side of his thinking, while Jung went on to develop his theory in the opposite direction. Religion is at the centre of the human experience, Jung (1948) argued, and that is why psychology cannot allow itself to neglect it. He stressed the need of many patients in "spiritual life," an ignorance of which "means faulty treatment and failure" (1933b, p. 224) and even claimed that the "prime evil" of neurosis is in disconnecting the individual from the religious heritage of humanity (1934, p. 172).

For many decades, psychoanalysis as an establishment judged harshly or ignored the phenomena Jung and his followers tried to connect with. However, since the beginning of the 21st century, the picture is changing. Concepts such as Bion's O turn from anecdotes to legitimate theoretical ideas. At the same time, there is a noticeable nearing between psychoanalysis and analytical psychology. At the 43rd congress of the International Psychoanalytic Association – held 90 years after the last congress attended by Jung – the dialogue between the two streams was officially renewed (Sandler & Giovannetti, 2005).

This transition in psychoanalysis occurred in parallel to similar processes taking place in Western culture, of growing sympathy to faith, especially in its "personal," non-organized expressions. The deep connection between psychoanalysis and prevailing cultural ideas and how it led to the rise of a spiritually sensitive psychoanalysis will be described in length in the next chapter.

Notes

1. In the same manner Freud found the origins of religiosity in infancy, other analysts traced the origins of Freud's anti-religiosity to his own childhood (e.g., Meissner, 1984; Rizzuto, 1998; LaMothe, 2002). Writing about Rizzuto's account, Esman (2003) observed she treated Freud's atheism just as he treated religion: "as a neurotic symptom" (p. 92).
2. Freud's criticism was part of a general attack on religion by Enlightenment thinkers. His favorite philosopher – as he told his colleague Eduard Silberstein in 1875 – was Ludwig Feuerbach (Gay, 1987), who argued that theology should be transformed into anthropology. In his chief work, *The Essence of Christianity* (1841), Feuerbach wrote that "the relation of reason to religion amounts only to the destruction of an illusion – an illusion, however, which is by no means insignificant, but whose effect on mankind, rather, is utterly pernicious" (quoted in Frie, 2012, p. 107).

    Another Enlightenment explanation of religion can be found in the writings of eminent sociologist Émile Durkheim. According to him, the enlightened rationalistic critique says that religion looks for an entity larger than man, which gives him power and which he has some possibility of communicating with – and claims such an entity doesn't exist. But exactly such an entity can be easily found – it is society itself. It is society which created man and it is society which supplies him with feelings of security. Society, according to Durkheim (1912), is the universal and eternal origin of religious feeling, which is nothing but the feeling society arouses in the individual, and which is projected outside of him or her and objectified.

Chapter 2

A very peculiar science
A brief cultural history of psychoanalysis

In the postscript to his *Autobiographical Study* Freud (1935) wrote: "My interest, after making a lifelong *détour* through the natural sciences, medicine and psychotherapy, returned to the cultural problems which had fascinated me long before, when I was a youth scarcely old enough for thinking" (p. 72). Psychoanalysis has long followed Freud's area of intellective interest, analysing culture using its complex theory. In addition to analysing it, psychoanalysis itself has had a tremendous effect on Western culture (e.g. Rieff, 1966; Parker, 1997).

Taking a reverse perspective regarding the "cultural problems" which fascinated Freud, that is, looking *at psychoanalysis* from a cultural point of view, provides a meta-analytic chart of certain major changes the discipline has gone through in the last century. In addition to profoundly influencing Western culture, psychoanalysis is also deeply influenced by it (e.g. Cushman, 1995). Specifically, psychoanalysis is influenced by the culturally prevalent Weltanschauung, which gives rise to common ambitions, as well as mental distresses, which psychoanalysis attempts to address in order to stay relevant to its patients. Beyond that, analysts too are products of the prevailing Weltanschauung, or "worldview" of their time. Seeing the world through its lens partly shapes their therapeutic approach, and especially their perceptions of "health" and "the good life."

Different psychoanalytic approaches thus hold distinct ideals and aims, drawn from the worldview prevalent at the time each approach developed. The claim is two-fold: psychoanalysis is influenced by socio-cultural *worldviews*; this influence can be observed in the changing formulations of psychoanalytic *treatment aims*.

Meltzer (1975) wrote:

> Psychoanalysis is such an essentially historical subject and method that it really doesn't make sense to talk about it any way but historically ... It's a very peculiar science that we have. I don't begin yet to understand how it works or develops and why sometimes it doesn't develop and sometimes it seems to shoot ahead.
>
> (p. 289)

In this chapter, I will describe these psychoanalytic developments, culminating in the development of Spiritually sensitive psychoanalysis, and locate them on the background of large cultural-historical trends regarding worldviews.

Historian Richard Tarnus (1996) defined "worldview" as "a set of values, of conceptual structures, of implicit assumptions or presuppositions about the nature of reality ... which constellate an entire culture's way of being and acting" (p. 34). This is in line with Freud's (1933b) definition in his *The Question of a Weltanschauung*: "[A] *Weltanschauung* is an intellectual construction which solves all the problems of our existence uniformly on the basis of one overriding hypothesis" (p. 158).

Hypotheses wide enough to answer *all* of our existential problems are few and far between. Freud claimed there are only five that fit his definition: the religious, the artistic, the scientific, the philosophical and the anarchistic worldviews. The list can be reduced even further. Taylor (2007) described three "perspectives," three ways of living and experiencing the world, that he claimed cover the whole range of human existence.

One perspective is the Religious. For those who hold it, according to Taylor, the place of "fullness" in life is always perceived as involving some search, recognition or service of goodness which exists *beyond* human life and nature (2007, p. 15).

Taylor's second perspective is secular, or "exclusive" Humanism. The "exclusiveness" lies in this perspective's notion of human flourishing, which "makes no reference to something higher which humans should reverence or love or acknowledge" (2007, p. 245). For those who hold to this perspective, the place of fullness is realized when we give our human reason primacy, and manage to live according to it.

The third perspective is called by Taylor "Neo-Nietzschean," more commonly recognized as "Postmodernism." This view denies the possibility of achieving any kind of Truth, be it religious or rational.

Because no perspective is perfect, or can be proven to be "correct," throughout human history an ongoing "three cornered battle" (Taylor, 2007, p. 636) could be seen as taking place between them. All three perspectives had adherents at every point of human history, and yet cultural processes lead to changes in which one enjoys cultural ascendancy at different times, a fact which also influences psychoanalysis.

Psychoanalysis was conceived as part of the scientific Weltanschauung (Freud, 1933b). In Taylor's terms, Freud's commitment could be understood to be to the Secular-humanist perspective, prominent at his time. This perspective holds to ideals of belief in humanity and its capacity to progress towards Truth using science. The underlying aspiration of Humanism is to scientifically re-order society and nature, to suit human purposes, taking into account the good of everyone, striving for universal justice and happiness.

The human being itself is perceived by Exclusive Humanism as a disengaged, disciplined agent, capable of remaking its self. According to this perspective, the power to reach a full and satisfying life, "a life worth living," lies within the person, as a *rational* agent.

Freud devised the psychoanalytic system and technique around these humanistic beliefs. The "one person" approach of classical psychoanalysis was described in medical, scientific terms. Freud's (1912) model was the surgeon, "who puts aside all his feelings, even his human sympathy, and concentrates his mental forces on the single aim of performing the operation as skillfully as possible" (p. 115). The doctor, Freud continued, "should be opaque to his patients and, like a mirror, should show them nothing but what is shown to him" (1912, p. 118).

This commitment was strengthened by Ego Psychology, which reached the height of its influence in the 1950s, especially in the United States. Ego Psychology thinkers called their theory "classic" and considered themselves dedicated followers of Freud (see Wallerstein, 2002). Their main contribution could be seen in the attempt to turn psychoanalysis into a *completely* positivist, objective and scientific endeavour. In addition, they put much more emphasis on the ego and its normal functioning (Lev, 2015).

Heinz Hartmann (1939a), the leading figure in this analytic school, emphasized its clear affinity to science: "The distinctive characteristics of a psychoanalytic investigation is not its subject matter, but the scientific methodology, and the structure of the concepts it uses" (pp. 4–5).

Like any scientific work, psychoanalysis was believed to lead to where the evidence takes it (Szasz, 1957) – not to where the researcher or subject might want it to go. Analysis was thus not perceived as aiming directly to change patients' mood, conduct or degree of happiness, but only at expanding their *knowledge* of themselves. Psychoanalysis is nothing but "a truth method," stressed Erikson (1969, p. 245). Eissler (1965) went as far as claiming that "[The] therapeutic coloring that pervades the psychoanalytic situation ... does not reflect the essentials of the psychoanalytic process" (p. 72).

Another characteristic of Ego Psychology was its consideration of normalcy and adaptation as central issues of psychoanalytic discussion. Freud's analytic psychology was focused on the unconscious drives that motivate behaviour. In contrast, in Ego Psychology the ego became central.

Not surprisingly, the emphasis on the ego was based on the *scientific* theory of evolution. Hartmann's (1939a) assumption was that ego evolved over millennia and so each human baby is born with ego-potentials that, under reasonable conditions, will develop and allow her to grow into a normal, adapted person. The goal of analysis therefore becomes to help the patient by strengthening her ego. This outlook suits the Humanist view of humankind.

Ego Psychology thus furthered Freud's "Humanist" outlook, both in its scientific attitude and in its focus on "normal," conflict-free elements. The Secular-humanist Weltanschauung's profound influence could be seen clearly while examining Ego Psychology's analytic aims. As Ego Psychology saw the analytic treatment as a scientific investigation of the patient's personality, it advocated as a central objective of analysis the discovery of Truth about the patient. Its second central goal was perceived as bringing patients to a state of relating adaptively to their reality, that is to the human culture and society around them. According to Wallerstein (1992), this goal was "the singular hallmark of the ego psychology perspective in psychoanalysis" (p. 69). This is in line with the Humanist perspective's ideal, as it was summarized by Taylor: "[it] take[s] the normalized ... for fulfilled human beings" (2007, p. 642).

The scientifically-oriented Humanist world-view lost power in the 1960s. The strengthening of feminism and sexual liberation, which followed the Civil Rights movement and responded, among other things, to the escalating nuclear arms race, eventually led to the rise, in the last quarter of the 20th century, of the perspective that Taylor called "Neo-Nietzschean," more commonly referred to as "Post-modern."

The term "Post-modernism" is a highly contested one, and there is no consensus as to what Post-modernism really means (Hassan, 2001). One of its central ideas, though, is an incredulity toward meta-narratives, a disbelief in absolutes and particularly in absolute Truth (Lyotard, 1979), including a scientific one. As Rustin (1999) put it: "The claims of reason, of science, of universal moral truths, and of a linear idea of historical progress, are put into question" (p. 105).

The claim is that there isn't, and couldn't be, one single, universal, explicable narrative, that there is no "absolute" and hence no one true rationality, no single morality or theoretical framework. As all knowledge is considered a cultural product, reflecting the values of the society where it was formed, there is no reason to give a specific set of ideas any preference.

The fact that post-modern society admitted to no common ideology or vision that could supply the individual with meaning and stability led to the common complaint of anxiety. In the new, "liquid" reality (Bauman, 2000) anything could change at any moment. This was true also, perhaps especially, in the most intimate sphere. The post-modern era was characterized by what Giddens (1992) called "the pure relationship" – a relationship formed only for itself, and preserved only as long as both parties find it satisfactory. The family unit changed accordingly. In 1993 a third of the children in the United States were born to an unmarried mother, compared with 5% half a century earlier. Of the two-thirds who were born to married parents, 45% were expected to see their parents divorce before they turned 18 (Fukuyama, 1999).

Something similar happened in the workplace. Whereas in the previous, "modern" era, the dominant script was of people gradually progressing in the corridors of a single workplace, two at the most, over their entire working life, at the end of the 20th century a college graduate was expected to change 11 jobs in at least three different areas during his or her career (Sennett, 1998).

This new situation affected large parts of the population, including those who continued to individually hold to a more traditional worldview. North Atlantic Civilization, Taylor (2007) wrote, "has been undergoing a cultural revolution" (p. 473).

Meta-narratives, social institutes and stable families and jobs all provided a sense of security and meaning. Without them, many people were left in a state of loneliness and loss. The post-modern era, negating singular concepts of truth, morality, meaning, etc., also had many advantages over previous eras of fundamental religious regimes, tyrannical ideologies, racism, conformism and sexual repression. Freedom from meta-narratives allows individuals to choose and form their life as *they* see fit. But it also created the option to fail at this new project. Each individual was given, or burdened with, great responsibility – to create and choose his life – whether he wants to or not. Self-exploration thus became the most important thing for many. Self-identity was not considered a "given" anymore but a "mission," a reflexively organized endeavour.

Psychoanalysis adapted itself to the cultural and social changes. In the first place, it became itself much more post-modern. The elements mostly influencing analytic discourse in the 1980s and 1990s were the post-modernistic focus on the constructed nature of analytic knowledge and criticism on the positivistic tradition of classical psychoanalysis (Bader, 1998). Psychoanalysts increasingly believed that reality is simultaneously created and found, constructed and revealed and, in the analytic setting, that the analyst's subjectivity and her theory influence what she sees and the meanings she finds and builds for the patient (Govrin, 2006).

Post-modernity became deeply entrenched in collective intellectual and cultural psyche and the post-modern era analyst focused too on blind spots and limitations of treatment. There is no truth regarding the patient, no one "right" choice or "correct" interpretation. For many analysts, the proper epistemology for psychoanalysis was no longer positivist but constructivist or perspectivist (see Elliott & Spezzano, 1996). Sass (1992) described this move as "a sea change" in the way therapists perceive their job (p. 167). Instead of seeing their profession as part of the scientific-medical world, Sass wrote, many of them started to refer to their work on the analogy of poetry or art.

The post-modern turn affected the entire psychoanalytic field, but it was most apparent within the analytic paradigm which fitted best the new Zeitgeist – that which emphasized object-relations and intersubjectivity.

The turn to the self led to change in the clinical picture. As Cushman (1994) wrote, unlike more discrete illnesses which tormented neurotic patients of the Freudian era, post-modern disorders were in fact long-term *adaptational strategies* whose symptoms emerged in interpersonal interactions. The typical patient in this era was devoid of specific symptoms and complained about "vague, diffuse dissatisfaction with life" (Lasch, 1979, pp. 80–81).

Narcissistic personality became perhaps the most common disorder of the era. As Benjamin (1988) noted,

"Narcissus has replaced Oedipus as the myth of our time" (p. 136).

This was tightly connected to changes in family structure. The emergence of the narcissistic character in the 1970s, Hale (1995) wrote, was a manifestation of the increasing instances of unresolved feelings of dependency upon the mother. The increasing dependency was explained by the shrinking of families (smaller number of children in each family), the weakening position of the father in the family, and rising divorce rates and growing numbers of families where the mother was the only caretaker – all factors that made relationships within the family, especially between mothers and children, closer and stronger. According to Hale (1995), the rise of object-relations theories in psychoanalysis was a direct outcome of these trends in family structure.

Starting with Ferenczi and Fairbairn, object-relations theories confronted some of classical psychoanalysis' basic premises, specifically Freud's instinct or drive theory. There are various object-related theories, all essentially emphasizing *relations* as the context in which the self develops. The yearning to form intersubjective constructions is described as a basic human need, beyond biological instincts and drives (Ogden, 2004).

This led to a change from "one person psychology," in which the mind of the patient, perceived as having an autonomous, independent existence, is the sole object of research, to a "psychology of two," in which the mind is perceived as essentially dyadic, social, interpersonal. In "two person psychology," transference and countertransference relationships, seen as a co-creation of analyst and analysand, become the centre of analytic process, since the assumption is that the patient's mind cannot be investigated separately from the intersubjective field (Aron, 1996).

While becoming more post-modern in its outlook and theory, psychoanalysis also sought clinically to accommodate itself to specific needs of its clients as they arose from the new reality. Especially, it addressed the desperate and often paradoxical need to rely only on oneself on the one hand and to escape from the intolerable feeling of loneliness and alienation by engaging in the intensive intimacy of "pure" relationships on the other.

All this comprised what was termed the "Relational Turn" in psychoanalysis. The relational paradigm, whose roots can be traced as far back as Ferenczi, thus gained popularity and vogue, which led to the development of new and successful variations, as was perhaps most apparent in the case of Relational Psychoanalysis. Relational Psychoanalysis was seen as a bridge between British-school object-relations theories and American Interpersonal Psychoanalysis (Mitchell, 1990). It arguably became the most dominant alternative to classical psychoanalysis in North America (Mills, 2005).

Relational Psychoanalysis adopted a perspectivist epistemic model (Aron, 1996), that fit neatly with the post-modern Weltanschauung. In addition, its clinical model, in which the basic unit of investigation is not the individual as a separate entity whose desires collide with reality, but a field of interactions in which the individual tries to create relationships and express himself, was very fitting to the personal aspirations and mental difficulties created or caused by the new prevailing worldview.

Another impact of post-modernism could be seen in new understandings of what was considered "pathological." Steven Mitchell (1993), one of the founders or the Relational school of thought, defined pathology not necessarily in terms of conflicts penetrating experience, as it was defined in classical psychoanalysis, but as a lack of richness to this experience. If for classical psychoanalysis the main treatment aims were gaining control over drives and the patient achieving a rational understanding of herself, in the late 20th century a more authentic, full sense of life became the central aim. If Freud and his Ego Psychology successors aimed at the normative, "natural" experience of love and work, later writers insisted on the ability to play and to create as expressing well-lived life. Normalcy turned from something to be aspired towards into a problem to be healed.

Psychoanalytic formulations of treatment aims thus followed cultural changes in perceptions of the good and meaningful life. Jurist (2000) differentiated two modes of being, "self-objectification" and "self-exploration," and described a "deep chasm" that opens up between what can be called "science of the self" and "aesthetics of the self" (p. 132). If the former characterizes classical psychoanalysis, the latter fits relational modes. Thus, normalcy, rationality and adaptivity were replaced by creativity, authenticity and a greater capacity to experience and live as the foundations of life worth living.

Yet the "three-cornered battle" went on. At the start of 21st century, many thinkers claimed the reign of postmodernism to be nearing its end. Linda Hutcheon, in the epilogue to the 2nd edition of *The Politics of Postmodernity* (2002) wrote clearly: "Let's just say it: it's over ... The postmodern moment has passed" (p. 166, p. 181). In its place, it seems we witness a resurgence of the religious perspective. This worldview responds to its predecessor's most keenly felt failings, namely the loss of a sense of security, which stemmed from changes in workplaces, in patterns of relations in the family and in community and society at large and the loss of a sense of meaning, as all truths were undermined by post-modern critique. Our sense of fullness, of having a fully lived life, argued Taylor (2007), is always a reflection of faith in some transcendent reality. This can explain why the religious is returning.

It is impossible to define "religion," as the phenomena included under this term are tremendously varied in human life. Yet for the purposes of the discussion here,

Taylor's (2007) suggestion that the essence of "religion" is faith in something transcendent could be sufficient.

Faith's return takes several forms. The fundamentalist form eases the heavy post-modern burden of having to choose alone each aspect of life, by shifting the locus of authority back from self to tradition. Another avenue of return is proposed by the popular New Age movement, which adds enchantment to a world left too grey by science and rationalism.

Here I focus on the third form of faith to arise lately, which I call "New Spirituality." This pattern of faith puts its emphasis on the inner, subjective experience, over traditional, more authoritarian forms. Simply put, while religion focuses on God (it is "God-centred"), spirituality focuses on the subject and his or her experience.

According to sociologists, the turn to spirituality dwarfs, in numbers, nearly every social movement of the past century. Sociologist David Tacey (2004) did not hesitate to say: "We are in the presence of a great historical shift, as the secular period which arose with humanism and the intellectual enlightenment draws to an end" (p. 18).

Forman (2004) estimated at the beginning of 21st century that 50–83 million Americans (19–32% of the population) held, to some extent, to spiritual ideas, and that the numbers are quite similar in all industrialized societies. Other figures point to the same conclusion: In 2001, 72 medical schools in the United States, more than half of all schools in the country, offered courses on spirituality and healing – compared to three schools that did so ten years earlier (Herrick, 2003); According to a study by the UN, one of every three tourists in the world is a pilgrim, to a total of 330 million people a year (Feiler, 2014); In 2007, 38% of United States residents were assisted by complementary and alternative medicine (Barnes, Bloom & Nahin, 2008); Three years later, more than six million

Americans have been helped with mind-body therapies such as yoga, tai chi, chi kung or meditation, following the recommendation of their doctors, along with an additional 35 million who have done so on their own initiative (Nerurkar et al., 2011).

The general nature of the cultural shift toward the spiritual has to do with the common *pattern* of faith, which is no longer organized "religion," as it has been for millennia. Even seemingly traditionally-religious people are more and more inclined to the "personal," spiritual aspects of their faith (Wuthnow, 2007; Heelas, 2008; Pew, 2012). This new pattern of religiosity, Taylor (2007) wrote, is "a shuttering development" (p. 514).

The distinction between two modes of faith was described already by William James (1902), who spoke of "[a] great partition which divides the religious field" (p. 30). On the one side of it lies "institutional religion," which stresses the divinity, and on the other "personal religion," which puts the individual at the centre.[1]

Today the same divide is described simply as one between "religion" and "spirituality." Whereas spirit is felt to be spontaneous, freely available and democratically structured, religion is perceived to be doctrinal, regulated and authoritarian (Tacey, 2004). In contrast to religion, spirituality holds that the sacred is intimate and close, directed to listening to the inward conscience rather than obeying external dictates of religious authority. According to it, "the way to God is through the self, not beyond the self or through pious disregard of the self" (Tacey, 2004, p. 81).

It should be noted that spirituality is not opposed to religion. "What divides godly and godless religion," wrote the philosopher Ronald Dworkin in his book *Religion without God* (2013), "is not as important as the faith in value that unites them" (p. 28). New Spirituality draws many ideas from established religions and their long-standing traditions, while at the same time the established religions themselves become more and more spiritual.

The religious Weltanschauung, currently on the rise, can thus be seen as one which supports the variety of religious phenomena. What lies at the deepest base of this world-view isn't the worship of God, or, on the other hand, the belief in the subject as possessing a transcendent potential, but – faith itself. This is a faith in the existence of some Good that exists beyond the human, natural life, a faith in the existence of some Reality beyond the immanent (Taylor, 2007).

Psychoanalysis, which is highly sensitive to changes in society and culture, seems to be responding to this shift in dominant Weltanschauung. While fundamentalism and New Age beliefs are still uniformly considered something to be analysed away, New Spirituality has allowed psychoanalysis to transform its relationship towards faith. This kind of spirituality isn't collective but personal and it sees faith as a *choice* an individual makes, not something one is born into. Even though the religious worldview was considered for many decades outcast in analytic circles, the fact that New Spirituality puts its emphasis on the inner, subjective experience has allowed psychoanalysis to incorporate some of its ideals as legitimate goals and expressions of a life worth living.

Freud's attack on religion can be understood as directed mainly towards its institutionalized forms. Once the prevalent mode of faith is perceived as inner and stops depending on society, church or organized religion, it fits better into the basic premises of psychoanalysis, as both psychoanalysis and spirituality are centred on awareness of personal experience, and aspire to support personal growth towards wholeness and authenticity (Stone, 2005).

These trends have led to a profound shift in psychoanalysis in the last two decades, expressed in a dramatic increase in publications on the spiritual dimensions of human existence (Lev, 2018). The stress for change in psychoanalysis comes from the side of patients: Simmonds (2004) found that analysands increasingly demand that their "spiritual issues" be treated with the same respect as any other subject they might bring into analysis and Rubin (2006) noticed that many prospective patients say in advance they are looking for a "spiritually oriented" analyst.[2]

But it isn't that analysts are cravenly bowing to their patients' demands from pragmatism: mainly, many of them share the change in patterns of faith (Roland, 2003). Samuels (2004a), who identified this trend, wrote, "I have no alternative but to count us as part of this general, worldwide resacralizing movement" (p. 824). After about two decades of spiritual-analytic investigation, this "movement" in psychoanalysis might be seen as a new emerging school within psychoanalysis – to which this book is dedicated.

Spiritually sensitive psychoanalysis isn't a dogma. All it offers is another option of looking at the self, and at the analytic process itself. This new sensitivity does not replace older ones but enriches them. The capacity to integrate sensitivity to the spiritual with the sharp clarity of psychoanalytic lens, could be seen as creating a new synthesis, which offers a fuller picture of the human condition and its potentials, and which can be relevant and beneficial for specific patients.

Being sensitive to the spiritual does not make one forget that faith can be at times regressive, encapsulated in primary narcissism, experienced in anal-sadistic terms or dominated by splitting (Etezady, 2008). In fact, understanding these pitfalls on the path of faith is becoming more detailed. As the spiritual side of life turned into a legitimate field of research, analysts are more and more capable of recognizing and treating pathologies of spirit (this will be discussed in more detail in Chapter 5).

Alongside the more nuanced recognition of the possible pathologies of faith, there is today also an acknowledgment of faith's potentially positive value. Psychoanalysis shows that like any other human activity and endeavour, a spiritual search can serve a variety of functions (Rubin, 2006). And like with any other human capacity, the analyst can be expected to help relevant patients learn to use their spiritual capacities in a more conscious, beneficial way. As Etezady (2008) remarked, faith doesn't have to be regressive and pathological, but can also arise out of a depressive position (and perhaps, as I will later show, even out of a still higher position).

Developing such faith is one of the unique aims of a spirituality-sensitive psychoanalysis. To the "science of the self" and "aesthetics of the self" (Jurist, 2000), spiritually sensitive psychoanalysis seems to add an option of "transcendence of the self."

In the process described in this chapter, psychoanalysis gradually widened the scope of ideals of mental health and of meaningful and satisfying life to whom people can aspire, and which it can help them fulfil. Each of the three world-views described offers a legitimate path to achieving a "full" existence in Taylor's (2007) terms. When the clinician is able to analytically approach each of them, with an understanding of both their value and of the unconscious motivations that can hide behind them, she can better analyse a wider variety of patients, through diverse periods in life. The worldviews incorporated over the years into psychoanalytic discourse do not have to come at the expense of each other, but can add in a "cumulative" way, as Rangell (2006) suggested.

In the ancient Jewish *Pirkei Avot* it is said that "[t]he world stands on three things: on Torah, on work, and on acts of loving" (1:18). These can be seen to represent the three Weltanschauungen described above, and if so, perhaps it can be said that today, with the inclusion of the spiritual, the psychoanalytic world stands more solidly as well.

In Part II of the book I will look more closely at this new "leg" that psychoanalysis stands on. I will chart what it adds to the analytic theory (Chapter 4), and how does it expand its treatment goals (Chapters 5 and 6).

Notes

1. Fromm (1947) distinguished, quite similarly, between "authoritarian" forms of religion, which are rooted in submission to authority, and "humanistic" religious experience and morality, which are based on a spirit of independence.
2. A classical psychoanalytic approach would see in such requests a kind of resistance, to be analysed and not acceded. Yet this demand can be seen as wholly legitimate. Sorenson (2004a) offered a provocative analogy: a holocaust survivor doesn't have to be analysed by a psychoanalyst who is a holocaust survivor herself, but can he go to therapy with an analyst who is a holocaust denier?

Part II

A spiritual model

Chapter 3

Religious instinct, sacred unconscious and the area of faith

Towards a new model of the psyche

At the beginning of the 21st century, more and more analysts see religion, faith and spirituality not necessarily as evidence of pathology, or as attempts to escape from unpleasant reality to illusion, but as possible expressions of deep and important parts of what it is to be human. Certain forms of faith and religious practice are evaluated as signifying healthy psychic development, that could be expected to emerge through a successful analytic process. Removing symptoms, adapting to reality or achieving greater capacity for intimate relationships, are no longer considered by spiritually sensitive analysts all that a person might aspire to through treatment.

Spiritual elements and ideas are becoming increasingly more prevalent in psychoanalytic articles, books and conferences. The spiritually sensitive stream of thought is indeed not at the centre of mainstream psychoanalysis, but in addition to the classic motifs of childhood sexuality, unconscious processes, resistance, repression and transference relations, spiritual tunes are getting louder and louder. Through the abundance of contemporary spiritually sensitive writings, by analysts such as Alan Roland, Ana-María Rizzuto, Cynthia Stone, Joseph Berke, Michael Eigen, Paul Marcus, Salman Akhtar and Stanley Schneider, as well as the late James Grotstein, Neville

Symington, Nina Coltart, Randall Sorenson and William Meissner, to name a few, a clear melody is emerging.

According to Govrin (2006), in order to be considered a psychoanalytic school, a new approach has to present a general theory of the human psyche that includes premises on stages of development, the transference relationship, the healthy personality, psychopathology and therapeutic goals.

In Chapters 4 and 5 I will expound on the unique therapeutic goals set by spiritually sensitive analysis, as ascribed by its view of the healthy personality. Before doing that, I will present in brief some of the premises that are set by this new tradition regarding the other basic theoretical issues, those of development, transference and pathology. In addition, I will expound in this chapter on a novel technique to approach the patient's unconscious.

The religious and the spiritual Weltanschauung is based on faith. In spiritually sensitive thinking, faith and belief gain renewed legitimacy within psychoanalysis, as essential aspects of healthy human existence and not illusory mental products. LaMothe (2002) claimed that "it is not possible to exist or live without faith" (p. 372). Rizzuto (2003) added that "'believing' is indispensable for the normal working of the mind and foundational for psychic life" (p. 2).

Of course, the necessity of faith doesn't mean all kinds of faith are psychologically similar. Even after the "spiritual-turn," analysts do not forget that faith can be a sign of pathology, compensation or defence. However, to that is now added the recognition that it can also arise out of the depressive position, and be therefore "reflective, objective, morally integrated, and transcendent" (Etezady, 2008, p. 562). Eigen (1981) wrote about such an *area of faith*, which is a way of fully being and experiencing, "with one's whole being, all out, 'with all one's heart, with all one's soul, and with all one's might'" (p. 413).

This capacity is thought to be accompanied by a specific instinct directed to its fulfilment. Bion told Grotstein (2006), who was his analysand, that he believes there exists a "religious instinct," which he considered to be as important as the libidinal, if not more (p. xiii). Similarly, Gordon (2006) claimed there is a basic human tendency to search for the numinous experience, and Marcus (2003) mentioned empirical research in the field of neurotheology, according to which a neurological circuit exists in the brain which mediates spiritual experience.

These human capacities, forces and potentials have been overlooked by mainstream psychoanalysis, as well as Western culture at large during most of the previous century. Consequently, as Fromm (1956) wrote, if in the 19th century the problem was that God is dead, in the 20th century the problem is that man is dead. The removal of the numinous from everyday life, which characterized the modern Western world, flattened a central dimension of self-experience. This is why the sense that there is a life-force missing "has become the ontological mood of our time" (Gordon, 2004, p. 6). What's missing, forgotten, added Eigen (2001b),

> is not *sub*, but *supra*. The over-world, oversoul, the All-Soul. Saturated by Lower, we tend to lose contact with the Higher. Filled with our ambition, passion, desire, survival care, weakness – God fades from view. The equipment God gave us to contact Him sinks into unconsciousness and is poorly used or misused.
>
> (p. 8)

Spiritually sensitive psychoanalysis stands against what Lawner (2001) called the "radical materialist project" which aspires to "reduce psyche to matter" (p. 553). It tries to broaden the psychoanalytic investigation from dealing with mind or consciousness alone, to referring also to "soul" or "spirit" as aspects of human existence. Freud himself often referred in his writings to the Soul (*die Seele*) of man as the object of his investigation, yet this word was systematically translated by Strachey as "mental apparatus," or similar "scientific" concepts.

Classical psychoanalysis' avoidance of anything spiritual could not last forever. *Seele* found its way back into psychoanalytic metapsychology through Winnicott's sacred incommunicado element, or through Eigen's descriptions of an a-material place in the psyche, "an indestructible I-kernel ultimately made of radiance" (Eigen & Govrin, 2007, p. 68).

The picture of the human being thus expands, to include "universal life" in addition to material and social life (Karasu, 1999, p. 143). Humans are social creatures, clearly, existing within a relational context, but we are also religious/spiritual creatures, as Eigen (1998a) wrote: "We are sustained directly by God, not only through others. We are sustained by others, not only by God" (p. 228).

This kind of thinking also permeates the understanding of transference relationships. The analytic knowledge of transferential and counter transferential dynamics is increasingly growing, but, as Tennes (2007a) argued, these advancements do not explain the mystery of *how* we know what we know – the mystery of how "a passing thought, a deeply felt affective state, or even a visceral reaction may lead us most directly to our patients' internal worlds" (p. 506). In order to embark on such an explanation she suggested a model in which self and other, subject and object, both are and are not separate – offering a radical leap that brings psychoanalysis into transpersonal territory (see also Brown, 2020). Quite similarly, Bar Nes (2021) referred to the mystical essence of daily analytic experiences such as transference, countertransference or projective identification.

Theoretical leaps of this kind allow spiritually sensitive analysts to settle within psychoanalysis ideas which have so far been considered foreign to analytic thought. Meissner (2008), for example, explained within an analytic model the Catholic idea of divine grace; Eigen (1998b) referred to the idea of the existence of the soul beyond the physical existence thus laying what could be considered a first foundation to a new expansion of psychoanalytic developmental theory:

> Contrary to so much analytic thinking, the first fall isn't from womb to birth. The great catastrophe isn't in going through the womb to getting born. The great catastrophe is going from heaven into the womb.
>
> (p. 199)

These emerging new ideas regarding the human psyche and soul could also broaden our understanding of the unconscious. Rubin (2006) wrote that Marx recognized the "social unconscious" and Freud the "personal unconscious," and wondered whether in the 21st century we should become aware of a "sacred unconscious." Getting in touch with this area of unconscious, he suggested, could lead to seeing "the world as more holy ... see[ing] it whole" (p. 149).

Paying attention to this kind of unconscious and its manifestations can be used in our practice and add to accustomed modes of doing therapy. In what follows, I will present an example to such a novel analytic technique.

Jungian analytical psychology is known for the emphasis it puts on synchronicity events. Jung's term refers to unique, spiritually laden occurrences in which two or more coinciding events are connected meaningfully but not causally. A famous example given by Jung (1952) is the appearance of a rare beetle in the consulting room just as his patient recalled a dream involving a similar beetle. The two events – the flight of the insect into the clinic and the recollection of the dream – are meaningfully connected but are not connected causally: the one did not make the second happen, and vice versa. Noticing the meaningful connection between events and exploring it often produce a profound therapeutic effect on patients, and have become a common technique used by Jungian analysts.

Another spiritually based avenue that one can use in analysis is to explore what I call "dream-like events" (DLE) (Lev, in press). Although these events are real, lived occurrences, it is possible to treat them like actual dreams, with significant clinical effect.

The central, defining element of the DLE is its symbolism: an external outside occurrence symbolizes a vital, often unconscious piece of mental reality. Symbolism is, as Freud (1900) stressed in *The Interpretation of Dreams*, one the central tools used by "regular" dreaming for representing their latent thoughts in a disguised way. As I will show, the DLE relies also on displacement (*Verschiebung*) and condensation (*Verdichtung*), "the two governing factors to whose activity we may in essence ascribe the form assumed by dreams" (Freud, 1900, p. 309).

Treating DLEs as we treat nocturnal dreams, I will suggest, gives us a new "royal road" to the unconscious, beyond the one famously cleared by Freud.

Being "dream-like," the events in question often have a surreal, fantastical or even uncanny quality, yet they are usually reported in an incidental manner, which suggests they are not the outcome of patients' projection of their inner life. In addition, even though their symbolism may seem exaggerated, almost fabricated, these reported events do not raise questions regarding the patient's reality testing.

These occurrences seem to be universal, even though some people are more perceptive of them than others are.

Religious instinct, sacred unconscious and the area of faith 49

With certain patients, an entire analysis can take place with few DLEs coming up or none at all, while with other patients they appear almost in every session. The analyst's receptivity is also crucial: if a patient reports DLEs and fails to evoke a substantial response, he or she will probably cease to do so.

The patient usually reports the DLE in a casual way, as something that happened recently, or as a recollection or association. The resemblance or connection to the patient's inner life is hidden from the patient, because of the unconscious element involved. However, after many such instances are recognized in the therapeutic discourse, some patients can make the connection between these events and their psychic reality by themselves.

To illustrate the character of these events, below I present two examples of DLEs taken from my clinical work.

The baby behind the wall. F. entered the clinic, and, as would often happen, fell into a long, burdensome silence. She could not say anything and obviously suffered for it. At some point she uttered, "Well, again!" After some minutes, she begged, "Help me, Gideon, please!" That meeting took place on the eve of New Year. I thought to myself that F. could comment about that and break the silence that she finds so burdensome. She didn't. Then, suddenly, she said, "My flat is divided into two – a big part, of four rooms, where I live, and a small part, consisting of one room. That one-room part had been occupied by two foreign women who came to Israel to work. After they left, a family arrived, with a baby. They also came from abroad to work. The landlord seems to me to be a "mafioso," he keeps bringing foreigners. The baby was crying and I thought – something should be done, why don't they do anything? He doesn't cry much, but at that moment, he cried." To my question, F. replied she never actually saw the baby: she shares a wall with the family, but never met them.

This minor incident reflected F.'s inner world and much of the work we were doing in therapy. In a marvellous display of condensation, the baby could be seen to represent F. herself, who had experienced a terrible tragedy, who cries for help, needs me, cannot soothe herself alone; it also represents a part of herself that she cannot reach, as it is blocked behind a wall, a part of her that cannot find its voice, hence "does not cry much"; in addition, the baby represents her own baby son, who died a violent death at a very young age, the baby F. cannot reach and help as she is blocked by the wall that separates the living from the dead. The physical wall in the flat can also be seen to symbolize the metaphoric wall that separates F., who is locked in the cell of her grief, from the world outside, from family life, even from me. Since the tragedy, four years ago, F. (herself an immigrant who moved to Israel a few years before her baby was born) disconnected herself from society – she quit work, hardly leaves the house and broke off all her relationships.

As we talk, F. has an association: when her baby was alive, F., her husband and the son lived in a small flat, "exactly like the one where the crying baby lives, precisely the same number of square meters." I say: "You stayed in that room, froze everything in your life." F.'s following association was that the landlord suggested that she move to the smaller flat, but she refused: "There wasn't a big difference in the rent." I took this association to reveal, unconsciously, that F. is beginning to be ready to leave the small cell of grief.

In the next session, for the first time, F. started talking the moment she sat down. She said she met the neighbours and the baby: "He is now a friend of mine." F. held him in her arms, the first time she had touched a baby since her son died.

Birds of love. In a session with K., I referred to the therapeutic relationship, and she dismissed my interpretation.

Religious instinct, sacred unconscious and the area of faith 51

I insisted that, in some way, what she talks about, though seemingly disconnected, often has to do with what happens in the clinic between the two of us. K. interrupted me before I finished the sentence: "I don't know why I am telling this, but yesterday I was at the central bus station – I don't like the place, it's filthy, physically as well as spiritually – and all of a sudden I heard birds. I looked around and saw two uniquely coloured parrots, lovebirds, *personatas* (this is the common name in Hebrew for the yellow-collared lovebird species, following the scientific name, *agapornis personatus*). The seller had them locked up in their cage. I asked him why, and he explained that he does this not as a protection against thieves, but because what these birds do, is that one opens the cage and the other escapes. I don't know why I told you this." I offered an interpretation: her association came after I talked about the relationship between her and me. It is indeed a beautiful symbol for therapy: two unique birds, personatas-personas, who meet in unpleasant circumstances (as patients almost always come to therapy when things get "filthy," literally and spiritually). One bird (the therapist) opens the cage for the other. K. was very moved, and so was I. This moment was a turning point in therapy that gradually allowed K. to acknowledge her feelings – both of being trapped in her caged-life, and of yearning to be freed and loved, by me.

Just like regular dreams, DLEs can have cognitive functions such as integrating new information acquired during the day with prior knowledge or regulating mood (Blechner, 2013). Psychic functions ascribed to dreams could be relevant to DLEs as well, and be fulfilled through them, just as they are achieved by regular night-time dreams. Such functions are fulfilment of a wish (Freud, 1900), compensation for excessively one-sided conscious attitude (Jung, 1948) or formulation of thoughts that could not be formulated in waking thinking (Blechner, 1998).

The Baby Behind the Wall DLE, for instance, communicates a message to the therapist that the patient could not find another way to deliver, as it involved material too painful for her to discuss directly. *Love Birds* can be seen to fulfil a wish of intimate connection with the therapist and liberation from the patient's difficult existence.

The fact that events that take place in real life at times tweak something inner and personal may seem odd. One possible explanation could be sheer coincidence. According to Littlewood's law (Littlewood, 1986), as each of us experiences tens of thousands of events each day of our life, it is statistically probable that once in a while we will encounter an event with odds of one in a million.

The "just a coincidence" explanation, very probably true for many DLEs, does not diminish the therapeutic potential of using them in analysis. Beyond that, after years of observing these events, it seems to me that sometimes something more might be involved than just chance. There are instances where the symbolic fit between the inner and outer seems too exceptional. How can we explain the fact that the flat beyond the wall was exactly the same size as the flat where F.'s son died? Or that the birds were not just any kind of parrots but specifically "lovebirds," their scientific name "personatas"?

The DLEs' uncanny nature alludes to a potentially mysterious, even mystical source. According to the mystic tradition, the outside and the inside are not sharply differentiated or completely separate. This is attested by mystics' "dreamlike images" (Hollenback, 1996, p. 231) which, at some exceptional cases, were proven to be precognitive or clairvoyant, that is, conveyed correct information about future events or events taking place at distant places (Mayer, 2007).

This brings to mind Bion's "O," which denotes the ultimate reality, a reality that cannot be known, but that it is possible to be at one with. This is a crucial observation, as, according to Bion (1970), "[n]o psycho-analytic discovery is possible without recognition of [O's] existence, at-one-ment with it" (p. 30). Hence, he concluded, what psychoanalysis requires is not a base for its theories or technique, but "a science of at-one-ment" (p. 88).

"O" represents the complete, total truth of reality. As such, it resides in all the myriad elements, events and objects that comprise this reality (Bion, 1970, p. 87). Each of these events and objects, in turn, being part of the unitary whole, reflects something of this ultimate reality. From our sense-based perspective, all events and objects seem to be separated, but these fragments are in fact "at-one" with the Whole and with each other. The outer and the inner, as well as the past and the present, only seem differentiated; in fact, there is no "in" nor "out," "now" nor "then," only parts of a Oneness which is beyond time and space.

This idea has some support in modern physics, for example in the work of the renowned theoretical physicist David Bohm (1980). As Bass (2001) claimed, "The most significant discovery of quantum physics is that there is a fundamental realm of unbroken wholeness underlying our perceived world of apparent separateness and fragmentation" (p. 695). DLEs can be seen to be expressions of this wholeness, eradicating the distinction between outer and inner, past and present.

Another approach that could be relevant to discussing DLEs may be found in Tennes' (2007a, 2007b) discussion of the "transpersonal" context in which she claims the analytic encounter takes place. The transpersonal dimension's characterizing quality is the meeting of "internal and external worlds … in a field of mutual interplay" (2007a, p. 519). Self and other are seen to be both separate and not separate, being parts of "a superordinate field that, however inadequate our capacity to explain it, informs and contains the analytic encounter" (p. 511).

This "field" is "an objective ground of being" (p. 514), "a fluid and unified whole" (p. 523).

When we recognize this field, Tennes (2007a) continued, "each moment, even the most seemingly prosaic, becomes part of such a whole, and the analytic relationship becomes a conduit for and participant in something much larger than itself" (p. 523). The moments of recognition in analysis "evoke awe," not simply because of their extraordinariness, but because they allow us, even if momentarily, to glimpse the possibility of this transpersonal field, "in which we are always participating" (Tennes, 2007b, p. 552).

Tennes talked about transpersonal events taking place in the transference relationship between analyst and patient, incidences where self and other are both separate and not separate. However, her formulation fits very well with DLEs as well, where inner and outer are revealed to be both separate and not separate. The concept of the transpersonal, quite similarly to that of "O," can give an explanation to the existence of these unique events of alignment between the personal and the factual, seeing them as coming out of the "objective ground of being."

The concept of the transpersonal can point to another major benefit of paying close attention to DLEs in analysis. Enhancing the patient's recognition of the "objective ground" can be of profound importance, as from the spiritually sensitive perspective offered by Tennes (2007a), the *purpose* of psychoanalytic work "is to transform the structures of subjective experience in a way that promotes the patient's alignment with what is objective in this ultimate sense" (p. 515).

According to the prevalent materialist view, objective reality is devoid of meaning. This view places us in an indifferent, disenchanted cosmos (Lev, 2016). Seeing outer reality not just as a chaotic, random blur of lifeless events but as somehow deeply connected to the inner self is a powerful tool when dealing with one of the most profound psycho-existential problems – that of meaninglessness (Becker, 1973; Yalom, 1980).

Mere existence and mere experience are intrinsically overwhelming. The human tendency, wrote Altman (2007) is therefor to render our experience "ordinary, not amazing, in the interest of making it manageable" (p. 532). Going too far with this tendency has a price of losing touch with the wonder of life, of existence. Observing DLEs, experiencing the outside reverberating the inside can give us back a sense of amazement, of meaning, even of awe, that has been lost in modern times. Eigen (2004) commented on Bion's work: "It is as if [he] says over and over: look, look, we are here, experiencing – we *experience*. Consciousness is dumbfounding, shocking. We are ALIVE!" (p. 42).

Dealing clinically with these peculiar events is challenging. We must learn not to treat them as purely subjective constructions, and at the same time, refrain from ascribing them a fixed, concrete meaning. As Tennes (2007a) wrote, "We are called on to hold the paradoxical recognition that we attribute meaning to our circumstance and simultaneously discover meaning within it" (p. 522)

This paradoxical position is playful in essence. Winnicott wrote about the "area of playing" that it is not inner psychic reality, yet it also does not belong to the outer reality: "It is outside the individual, but it is not the external world" (1971, p. 51). It is almost as if Winnicott (1971) was describing the DLE:

> Into this play area the child gathers objects or phenomena from external reality and uses these in the service of some sample derived from inner or personal reality ... In playing, the child manipulates external phenomena in the service of the dream and invests chosen external phenomena with dream meaning and feeling.
> (p. 51)

To this Winnicott (1971) added: "It is in playing and only in playing that the individual child or adult is able to be creative and to use the whole personality, and it is only in being creative that the individual discovers the self" (p. 54).

Before concluding the chapter, I will add one more DLE. M. was the patient who taught me more than any other about DLEs. Each session with her was an abundant source of fascinating true tales of unconscious symbolism, and our work on them led to a profound transformation in her life.

In the last moments of our last meeting, she told me one more story about a beloved horse she had as a child: "It was a stormy night. My 'dear' mother tied Sussy to a tree in the orchard. I knew horses are very sensitive to cold, yet was uncertain whether I should go out or not, because it was such a terrible storm. I was 10 or 11. Eventually I went out. It was dark. It's not like here, in the city, with lampposts spreading light. Total darkness, I couldn't see a thing. I didn't know how I could find her in the orchard. I cried 'Sussy!' and she replied 'hee-hee-hee!' This is how I found her. I untied her and we walked back. Often when we walked, she would put her head on my shoulder and follow me. I put her in the stable and went home to bed."

This story, a story about a horse, sensitive to the cold, that "dear," not-good-enough mother tied, and that was rescued in the stormy dark night by little M., a story that ended our last meeting, I heard as a creative-playful expression of a real event, dream-like, whose topic was exactly what Winnicott talked about, what we strive for in our best moments: discovery of the self.

Discovering the self through the outside world, reconnecting with amazement, are some of the goals of spiritually sensitive psychoanalysis. In the next two chapters I will expound on a few more.

Chapter 4

God-representations, mystical addictions and spiritual bypasses

Adaptive treatment goals

Psychoanalysis used to hold only a critical, reductive approach towards religion. But lately one can find two other approaches: adaptive and transformative (Parsons, 2007). Indeed, only the latter makes room for a truly spiritual dimension of the personality and the therapeutic process, but even the adaptive approach represents a change in the way psychoanalysis sees spirituality.

An "adaptive" psychoanalytic approach to faith, which doesn't reduce it to pathology, projection or wish-fulfilment on the one hand but also isn't openly spiritual in itself on the other, refers to the spiritual experience as any kind of human experience, which psychoanalysis can improve and intensify. Psychoanalysis, in this sense, is not perceived as aspiring to directly contribute to spiritual growth, but as a possible means to enable analysands to experience more fully the wide horizon of human existence, which also includes the transcendent (Shafranske, 2005).

Although not being inherently spiritual, the "adaptive" contribution could be of value to the spiritual patient. Mystical writers from various religious traditions noted that spiritual growth requires or invites a rigorous encounter with oneself. If psychoanalysis is not practiced in a reductionist and anti-spiritual manner, such an encounter is exactly what it can enable (Rizzuto, 2003).

One of the central spiritually adaptive changes an analytic therapy can promote is in regard to the patient's God-representation. Rizzuto (1979) described God, from the point of view of the individual, as an "object," which can have different representations in the human psyche. These representations, in turn, determine the object-relations the person has with his or her God. In this respect, spiritually sensitive psychoanalysis is not interested in the question of the psychological sources of the divine object (this is the classical Freudian approach), and neither in the question of the ontological status of God (this is the theological approach). Rather, relations with God are perceived as any form of object-relations, which are to be understood and transformed in the analytic process. De Mello Franco (1998) declared: "The representation of God brought by each analysand at the beginning of the analytic process is not the same as the one he arrives at when it is over" (p. 127; see also LaMothe, 2009). The question is how we experience God, wrote Ulanov (2000), whether in a lively and positive way or in a rigid, dead way.[1]

Another "adaptive" avenue is recognizing and treating spiritual pathologies. Being spiritually sensitive does not mean one evaluates positively every expression of faith. Indeed, as analysts become more nuanced in their approach to spirituality, so the psychoanalytic literature becomes richer in descriptions of problematic spiritual patterns, and deals more seriously with what Samuels (2004b) termed "the shadow side" of spirituality. Rubin (2006), for instance, who treated a large number of Buddhists, yoga practitioners and spiritual seekers, described a wide range of "pathologies of spirit" he identified. These include using the spiritual quest to narcissistically inflate oneself, to evade subjectivity or to deny emotional losses. All these can be tackled and altered in analysis, to enhance a truer spiritual path and not in order to block it altogether.

Similarly, Caplan (2009) mentioned the spiritual pitfall of identification of the ego with spiritual experiences and achievements. Such an identification might lead to spiritual pride and superiority, or to what she called "the chosen-people complex" – the belief that the spiritual group one belongs to is more spiritually evolved, powerful and enlightened than any other group.

In addition, Caplan (2009) spoke of confused motivations in spiritual seekers. Even in cases where the desire to grow is genuine and pure, it often gets mixed with lesser motivations, including the wish to be loved, the desire to belong, the need to fill internal emptiness or the belief that the spiritual path will remove all suffering. These might also lead to spiritual ambition – the wish to be special, to be "the best" – which contradicts the essence of spirituality.

Eigen (1998b) mentioned that the ecstatic spiritual experience itself can become dangerous – if there is a split and animosity between my "perfection" and yours (which characterizes fundamentalism). Mystical experience, he added, can even become addictive, perhaps even more than other, common addictions.

Moreover, Eigen (1998b) noticed some people use mystical experiences to bypass or blur a painful reality – the person focuses on the moments of elation, instead of working on his or her personal difficulties. In this sense, he wrote, certain mystical moments "are akin to being in the goal region without going through the maze" (p. 111). In the same line, Rubin (2006) noted that the spiritual path allows devotees to engage in masochistic surrender, schizoid detachment and obsessional self-anesthetization or to a pathological mourning of traumatic experiences. Psychologist Robert Masters (2010) added some more aspects of "spiritual bypassing," such as overemphasis on the positive, anger-phobia, blind or overly tolerant compassion, weak or too porous boundaries, devaluation of the personal relative to the spiritual, and "delusions of having arrived at a higher level of being" (p. 2).

The deep understanding of the pitfalls and pathologies of spirituality should not hide the big difference between the reductionist traditional approach and the present-day adaptive one. The adaptive approach, while recognizing the dangers of spiritual involvement, also notices its potential value. Like any other human activity, the spiritual search can serve a variety of functions, "ranging from the adaptive and transformative to the defensive and psychopathological" (Rubin, 2006, p. 140).

The "adaptive" analytic approach to spirituality can thus help patients use their spiritual capacities and fulfil their spiritual tendencies in better ways then they do currently. Analysis serves here as a tool to recognize and treat unconscious psychic forces which harm or distort the spiritual experience of patients, just as it does with any other human experience.

Note

1. Using this line of thinking, Spero (1992) tried to make room for the existence of "a real God" and not only a "god," which is an object-representation. According to Spero, there are indeed relations with God which involve projection, but that is true also with relations with the mother, for example. God *exists*, Spero claimed, just like the mother exists.

Chapter 5

Morality, selflessness, transcendence

Transformative treatment goals

The "adaptive" approach discussed in Chapter 4 probably encompasses the majority of analytic work done today in the spiritual context. However, the writings of spiritually sensitive thinkers also include "transformative" goals, that actively seek to achieve a change in patients' spiritual lives. These will be discussed in the current chapter.

One such transformative goal has to do with moral issues. Psychoanalysts have tended historically not to refer to morality as an important element in therapy. As Smith (1986) observed, the conventional vocabulary of moral deliberation is largely alien to the psychoanalytic lexicon. Words like "moral," "ethical," "virtuous," "righteous" and their opposites, seldom appear in clinical dialogue or in theoretical analytic writings.

In the early stages of the development of psychoanalysis, it distanced itself from "soul-centred" practices, and many analysts thought there was no point to investigate the ethical development of the person (Schaler Buchholz, 2003). If a patient expressed a will for a moral action, it usually led to a discussion of the hidden motivations behind this wish. Even in object-relational and intersubjective contexts, moral values remained a completely subjective matter. If a patient brought to therapy a moral question, the analyst would usually take, unconsciously, a one-person psychological perspective, and ask, "what do *you* feel, or want, or need?" and not "what is right?" (Rubin, 1997).

The emergence of spiritually sensitive psychoanalysis changed the picture around this issue. Analysts increasingly espouse a different understanding, according to which a search for moral attitude and values is an essential part of being human, and thus that it is essential also to psychic well-being. Coltart (1992) claimed straightforwardly that aspiring to virtue leads to happiness, and this is where therapy should aspire. Hadar (2013) agreed, stating "it is healthy to be good."

Such approaches are basically pragmatic. According to them it is important to consolidate a moral attitude because it helps the patient live a better life, giving him or her meaning and direction. A more radical view anchors morality in a realm beyond the pragmatic. Goodness becomes a goal in itself, and not a means. Eigen (2007) voiced a spiritual perception regarding the evolution of humanity towards the *Good*, that psychoanalysis is itself a part of. From this perspective, he advocated the ideal of "incarnating goodness" in daily living – even at the expense of personal well-being: "To evolve towards life in which we affirm one another's worth – infinite worth – entails sacrifice of well-being, ease, inertia. True self-esteem depends on it" (p. 21).

Psychoanalysis could be seen as nearing religion here, even relying on it. In itself psychoanalysis, whose origins are rooted in biological sciences, cannot identify, or supply, an adequate base for a sense of values (Black, 2006). Spiritually sensitive psychoanalysts thus look for compatibilities between psychoanalysis and religious or spiritual traditions. Stone (2005), for instance, connected the Christian and Jewish "love thy neighbour" with Kohut's "ever widening circle of concern." Berke and Schneider (2003), to take another example, compared psychoanalytic concepts with Jewish-Kabbalistic concepts like *Tshuva* (repentance) or *Tikkun* (which has been compared to the Kleinian "reparation").

Another source of influence for the search for moral excellence as part of the analytic ideal is the Buddhist concept of Compassion, which stresses that the compassionate concern for the needs of the other, not less than self-fulfilment, is considered part of a full and meaningful life. The psychoanalyst Jeffery Rubin (2004) emphasized that this means universal, and not only local compassion – the circle of concern should embrace more of humanity than only the person's family and friends.

The inclusion of advanced morality in the goals of psychoanalysis involves an attempt to differentiate theoretically between the super-ego, rooted in the classic perception of psyche, and the more spiritual "conscience." Symington (2004) criticized Freud's narrow approach to the latter, and claimed that unlike the super-ego (which is an internalization of outer authority), conscience serves as an inner guide to right action, the "right" action being that which "will ennoble both the self and the other." (p. 30).

The new analytic approach to morality constitutes a profound alteration regarding the perception of mankind and of the ideal of life. Psychoanalysis went through a shift from the epistemic demand of "know thyself" to the realm of the Ethic (Kulka, 2020). One might say that spiritually sensitive psychoanalysis adds to the common paradigms touching on the state of man – Freud's "guilty man" (forever struggling to satisfy his desires), Kohut's "tragic man" (struggling to realize the goals of his core self) and object-relations' "dependent man" (struggling to preserve relations with important others) – a fourth paradigm of "sacrificing man," struggling to maintain responsibility and compassion for the other, and for whom altruism and loving-kindness are the basic principles of living.

Of course, sacrifice is not the ideal, but the predicament (just like "guilt"). Spiritually sensitive psychoanalysis tries to enable the conscientious patient develop an altruistic stance arising not from blame but from responsibility and experienced not as painful but as joyful.

Developing responsibility and a sense of deep compassion involve a lessening of the boundary between the person and others, yet not at the expense of oneself. After all, the universal dictum demands *love thy neighbor as thyself.* Fromm (1950) remarked: "Love is based on an attitude of affirmation and respect and if this attitude does not also exist toward oneself, who is after all only another human being and another neighbour, it does not exist at all" (p. 87). How to develop self-love without falling into narcissism is related to another transformative goal of spiritually sensitive psychoanalysis, which concerns the place given to the self or "I."

One of the only assumptions common to all analytic approaches (perhaps excluding the Lacanian) is that every human being "has" a self. Each analytic school holds its own perception of this self, but always it is viewed as some kind of entity, with its own individual, independent, separate existence, which is what is explored in analysis. Spiritually sensitive psychoanalysis suggests an alternative to this basic perception.

As is well known, Freud and Breuer (1895) spoke about the "common unhappiness" (p. 305) of being. A main cause for this unhappiness, overlooked by psychoanalysis, could be the feeling of the self as isolated, encapsulated, which leads to focusing on the self and to some degree of narcissism. Narcissism can be thought to lie at the root of much of our psychic discontent. Symington (1994) even went as far as claiming that "[n]early all psychopathology has its origin in narcissism" (p. 126). Beyond personal suffering, the narcissism of the isolated individual leads to social ailments and to intolerance, inequality and injustice (Rubin, 1997).

Psychoanalysis is not to blame for the emergence of narcissism or its outcomes, but its "self-centred" concepts and theories might hinder the release of the individual from exaggerated self-focusing (Epstein, 1995). In overemphasizing a reified, egoistic individualism, psychoanalysis promotes excessive self-centredness and neglects other possibilities and features of subjectivity such as self-transcendence or non-self-centred modes of being.

One could assume that excessive preoccupation with the self will dissolve as a natural consequence of the patient's becoming more aware of and in touch with feelings and needs, his own and those of others – which is what is done in traditional analysis. But if therapeutic focus is almost exclusively put on the self, if autonomous, differentiated identity is viewed as the apex of human development and if non-self-centred modes of being are interpreted as symptoms of psychopathology – as is usually the case with traditional psychoanalysis (Rubin, 1997) – narcissism and preoccupation with self are unlikely to diminish as an outcome of therapy.

Looking for a way out of the narcissistic puddle, more and more analysts turn to spiritual traditions, such as Buddhism, which help it become less self-centred and less focused on the needs and wishes of the separate self.

According to Buddhism, the most basic human instinct, even more than sex and aggression, is the "intrinsic reality instinct" – the tendency to find an inner absolute essence to people and things. This is why we believe our self is totally real, and that we and others, have self-identity (Epstein, 2001). Modern physics teaches us this is not so, that nothing has a constant, independent existence, not even at the basic level of sub-atomic particles (Rovelli, 2021). But the reality instinct is deeply entrenched in our psyche.

The greatest contribution of Gautama Buddha was perhaps the assault on the paradigm that comes out of this basic instinct, a paradigm that views humanity as fundamentally self- and ego-centred. His main insight, consequently, was that a narcissistically invested, stable, permanent, separate self is imaginary, "a false belief which has no corresponding reality" (Marcus, 2003, p. 51).

This view is very distant from the Western perception of self. But as interest in spirituality and specifically in Buddhism is increasing, it is gradually penetrating Western discourse, including the psychoanalytic one. Many analysts involve personally in Buddhist practices (Lev, 2015), and are trying to reconcile the Buddhist approach to self with analytic theory. Such attempts offer, as an alternative to the common perception of a person who is the owner of a "self" or an "ego," a meta-narrative in which not the ego, but a lack of it is at the centre (Marcus, 2003). Similarly, one can find descriptions of a temporary and transitory self, which is wholly interdependent and impermanent, a self which is a "function" and not a "thing" (Young-Eisendrath, 2008), or of a self which is "empty," that is – without an experience or observer permanently set up in the background to watch all that goes by (Magid, 2000).[1]

In contrast to Winnicott's "true" inner self or Kohut's "nuclear self," the Buddhist true self is "no self," that is "the non-self-centered response to life as it is, the non-dualistic, non-essentialized experience of *being just this moment*" (Magid, 2000, p. 522). There is no "true" self, it is argued, because there is no true essence – to anything. Everything changes, all the time, including the self. Thus, there is only the self of this moment, which is as true or false, as any other self. Psychoanalyst and Zen teacher Barry Magid (2000) quoted the famous saying of 13th century Zen master Dogen, "Body and mind dropping off," and tried to give it a modern psychological interpretation:

> [W]hat drops off is the self-centered perspective of the isolated mind, that is, the perspective of someone who believes his or her self to be essentially private,

interior, autonomous, and separate. What remains is nothing extraordinary, simply a self no longer at odds with itself or the world. The no-self is not structureless or boundaryless in any usual psychoanalytic sense. Rather, it is fluidly, spontaneously, and meaningfully engaged with life.

(p. 523)

The ideal of "no self" is not only a consequence of Buddhist influence. Mystical techniques from all traditions aim at denying the self or losing the self, as means to face excessive self-interest, which leads to suffering and limits the capacity to love (Klein, 2004). Self-emptying (*Kenosis*) is a Christian ideal of mental health (Sorenson, 2004b), and a state of self-emptying is also described from a Jewish context (Eigen, 2001b).[2]

The attempt to "empty the self" is indeed new to psychoanalysis, but it should not be seen as standing in stark contrast to the more common analytic attempt of enhancing self-fulfilment or awareness. One can speak of two poles that spiritually sensitive psychoanalysis navigates – one of increasing self-awareness, another of diminishing preoccupation with the self. Perhaps it will be helpful here to distinguish between "self" as a process and never a "thing," which is what is enhanced, and "ego" which *in this sense* is the reification of an aspect of one's self, clung to out of anxiety or insecurity, and therefore waiting to be let go of.

This distinction was assimilated into psychoanalytic theory through the concept of surrender, which Ghent (1990) presented as a life-goal. According to him, the state of surrender is an experience of "being 'in the moment,' totally in the present, where past and future, the two tenses that require 'mind' in the sense of secondary processes, have receded from consciousness" (p. 111).

While in the West the concept of surrender has connotations of "defeat," in the East it is perceived as a method of transcendence as a result of the letting down of defensive barriers. Similarly, while in the West "ego" is associated with the individual's strength, rationality and selfhood, in the East "ego" is nothing but an illusion. Surrender is letting go of this illusion.

According to Ghent (1990), the human need for surrender is universal, and expressed in different ways in different cultures. In the West, the yearning for surrender is sometimes expressed in creative ways, but more often it is expressed pathologically. Masochism, for instance, could be understood as an unsuccessful expression of the wish for surrender (and not necessarily as a defence, as it is usually understood). Ghent suggested that psychoanalysis could offer an adaptive way to realize this need for release from a too tight attachment to an ego that is nothing but an illusion – the analyst serving as a replacement for the Eastern guru as the object of surrender. Thus, the transference-relationship can be used to reduce attachment to oneself.

Similarly, immersion in selflessness in the meditative experience, historically viewed by psychoanalysts as "a narcissistic-masochistic affair" (Alexander, 1931, p. 131), is found by spiritually sensitive analysts today to have potentially profound positive effects, both for the analysand, and for her relations with others. According to this view, the process of becoming more distant from the self does not lead necessarily to disconnection from reality, as perhaps the common image of a secluded Buddhist monk might suggest, but quite the opposite. As barriers between self and not-self erode, noticed Rubin (2006), "one feels a self-expansive connectedness with the world characterized by a sense of engagement, not escape or detachment" (p. 137).

In the same line, even though the Christian *Kenosis* means "self-emptying," it is different from "emotional absence." The Christian thinker Thomas Moore wrote:

"Jealousy empty of ego is passion. Inferiority empty of ego is humility. Narcissism empty of ego is love of one's soul" (quoted in Sorenson, 2004b, p. 458). Fromm (1966) too wrote that "*x* experience," in which the ego is transcended, is characterized by "making oneself empty in order to be able to fill oneself with the world, to respond to it, to become one with it, to love it" (p. 59).

Spiritually sensitive psychoanalysis thus offers a variety of unique ways to relate to the self: Zen-influenced approaches see the self as non-existent and claim the person has to acknowledge that; mystically influenced approaches see transcending the self, and not eliminating it, as a high spiritual achievement and a way to touch the numinous; while other approaches, like those of Ghent (1990) or Fauteux (1997), see the elimination of the ego-self as a way to reach another, truer self. Despite the dissimilarities, all of these approaches share a view essentially different from the accepted psychoanalytic stance as regards ego or self: in addition to seeing it as something that can be understood, empowered or developed, they see it as something that needs *also* to be essentially given-up, transcended or recognized as an illusion. This addition is for them a condition for greater psychic health, and thus a central goal of psychoanalysis.

So far, I have discussed spiritually sensitive analytic goals in the inter-personal (moral) and the intra-personal (changing the relation to the self) contexts. These ideals do not necessarily contradict earlier world-views upon which psychoanalysis was based. Even the most devout positivist will not argue against universal compassion and responsibility towards others, and will probably also find interest in doubting the mere existence of the self (e.g. Hood, 2012; Deacon, 2012; Oliver, 2020).

In this sense, the goals of increasing compassion or of diminishing self-focus, even if they are new to psychoanalysis, do not herald a Kuhnian "paradigm shift."

However, the third transformative goal, which will be described below, completely deviates from customary analytic discourse.

In fact, the goal itself is to "deviate" – from the immanent, material world of the senses. The aspiration is to what Rudolph Otto (1917) called "the numinous." According to Otto, the religious experience is an independent stream in the psychic life of humans, which cannot be reduced to psychological drives or to physiological needs. It is a category that is not drawn from the realm of normal everyday experience, and does not apply to anything natural.

Experiences of this kind are usually described as "mystical." Dan (1993) pointed out how difficult it is to define mysticism, but if we rely on Russell (1917), there are four basic points that mystics of various traditions agree on. The two points most relevant for the current discussion are the belief that there is a method of perception that is based on revelation, insight or intuition, and through which one can perceive a Reality beyond the world of phenomena, and the belief in Unity, which informs a refusal to acknowledge the existence of oppositions or divisions anywhere.[3]

Philosophers like Kant (1781) and Wittgenstein (1921) claimed that there is no possibility of a direct contact with such Reality or Unity. We humans necessarily perceive everything through our own categories (headed fundamentally by the categories of space and time) and through language, and this is why our reality is, to a large extent, a constructed one, and not a reality which represents "what's truly out there."

Mysticism claims to transcend these limitations and touch reality beyond the merely constructed. In the face of years of scientific, as well as psychoanalytic doubt, some researchers claimed there is evidence of cases in which unique experiences indeed supplied mystics with objective knowledge they had no access to, which refutes reductionist arguments (e.g. Hollenback, 1996; Mayer, 2007).

Other researchers described as mystical such human experiences that cannot be said to be determined, created or influenced by the person or by the context of their experiencing. Such "Pure Consciousness Events" (Forman, 1999) are states in which the person experiences Consciousness per se. After erasing all contents of consciousness, the mystic is left with clear consciousness itself, which is beyond the world of senses and matter (a state which is reminiscent of the ideal of self-emptying).

A third type of mystical experiences is of unity, the kind Romain Rolland described to Freud (1930) and which was explained by the latter as regression to the sensation of non-differentiation felt at infancy. Merkur (1999) tackled Freud's reductionist theory of oceanic feeling, using infant-observation research that showed that there is no developmental phase of primary narcissism, monism, or subject-object nondifferentiation, in which infants naively mistake their care-givers for parts of themselves.

Experiences of pure consciousness or of union were introduced into psychoanalysis by Fromm's "*x* experience," mentioned earlier, and more significantly by Bion's "O". This concept does not fall in the domain of knowledge or learning, as it "can be 'become', but it cannot be 'known'" (1970, p. 26). Hence it is impossible to explain exactly what "O" *is*. And yet, looking at Bion's associations to the concept might give an impression of what he meant by it. Writing of "O", Bion mentioned Kant's unknowable thing-in-itself, Platonic Forms, first cause, ultimate reality, absolute truth, the godhead, the infinite. In his mind, "O" awoke lines such as Dante's: "Eternal Light, that in Thyself alone/Dwelling, alone dost know Thyself, and smile/On Thy self-love, so knowing and so known!" (quoted in 1965, p. 138).

Recognizing "O", or being in "O", or being-"O" can be understood as another state of consciousness or human position in relation to reality. To the two classic Kleinian positions, the paranoid-schizoid position and the depressive position, a third, transcendent position could be added. This position describes, according to Grotstein (2000), the "state of serenity that accompanies one who finally, after traversing the nightmares of the paranoid-schizoid position and the black holes and mournful inner cathedrals of the depressive position, is able to become reconciled to the experience of pure, unadulterated Being and Happening" (p. 282).

The most prominent speaker in contemporary psychoanalysis for transcendence and mystical experience as legitimate objects of research and ideals of life is probably Michael Eigen.[4]

One of Eigen's main messages is that psychoanalysis has to acknowledge the existence of the mystical sensation, which is "a real force or forces, working in ways we barely sense" (1998b, p. 23). He even claimed (1998c) that psychoanalysis is in essence the science of ultimate reality of the personality, that is, of "O".

Over the years, Eigen tried to more fully define the mystical experience as a lofty sensation, yet one that is not disconnected from daily life and emotions (see Gordon, 2006). One of the mystical experiences Eigen (2001b) described is an experience of Light. In his words: "There is a Light of lights, and when one sees it no questions remain. There is nothing more beautiful" (p. 35). He does not seek to resolve the mystery of existence, but to celebrate it. One of the goals of life according to him is to be aware of the wonder of simply being alive.

The wonder, the mystery and the light stem from two sources. One stream gushes forth from the innermost depths within, from the unconscious. The second source is a transcendent being. Eigen (1981) argued against the reduction of the individual's perception of God to nothing more than transference, displacement or projection of parental figures as offered by Freud (1910) or Rizzuto (1979).

Experiences of Light, or "x," or "O," points of contact with the numinous, with God, are all part of what a spiritually sensitive analysis considers to constitute a life worth living. But how can one cultivate such experiences within the analytic context? Human language, wrote Bion (1992), suits only the description of the rational, and this is why it cannot touch that "force" that the mystics sensed, and which "cannot be measured or weighed or assessed by the mere human being with the mere human mind" (p. 371). How can the un-sayable be reduced to theory, to technique, be settled with the "talking cure"?

At this stage in the development of spiritually sensitive psychoanalysis there is no full answer. In fact, there will probably never be. However, one important way that psychoanalysis might assist in this search of the miraculous is by doing what it knows so well to do – remove resistances. Bell (2009) wrote: "it is the *overcoming of resistance*, not the knowledge of facts, that is at the core of the psychoanalytic understanding of psychic change" (p. 344).

Form the spiritually sensitive point of view, everything that psychoanalysis usually puts under "psychoneurosis," could be considered to ultimately constitute substitutions or screens for the experience of "O" (Grotstein, 2000). To id, ego and super-ego resistances, we need to add "O-resistance" which explains why even though people want nothing more than what is real – something or someone real – they also fear nothing more than what is real (Eigen, 1998b).

Discovering and working-through "O-resistances" enables and enhances the capacity to be mystically involved in the world. And this, as Marcus (2003) put it, "is a highly desirable state of mind to cultivate for the average analysand" (p. 31).

Notes

1. As mentioned, Lacan is one of the single analysts who talked about "no-self" before the spiritual-turn in Western culture. Moncayo wrote about the connections between Lacanian psychoanalysis and Buddhism, and claimed that for both "true self is no-self" (1998, p. 383).
2. The great 18th century Hassidic Rabbi, Baal Shem Tov, interpreted Moses' saying from the *Book of Deuteronomy* (5:5) "I stood between the Lord and you at that time" as meaning that "I," that is, the perception of self, a perception that there is an "I" who has a separate existence, is what stands between the person and God.
3. The other two points are denial of the reality of time and a belief that any expression of evil is an illusion.
4. Eigen even described his theoretical milieu, as "a budding subculture of psychoanalytic mystics" (Mitchell & Aron, 1999, p. 1).

Part III

Essential spirituality

Chapter 6

The window is the absence of the wall

Psychoanalysis as a spiritual practice

Psychoanalysis, Freud (1923) wrote, isn't one "thing," but three: a procedure for investigating the processes of the mind, a treatment devoted to ameliorating the ailments of the mind, and a general theory of the mind. But it is also one more, essential, thing. As I will demonstrate in this chapter, psychoanalysis is also a spiritual activity and even a spiritual practice.

So far, I have shown how psychoanalysis has become more sensitive to the spiritual, and how this has affected its theory, technique and treatment goals. Yet there is another aspect to this issue: there are spiritual characteristics that can be found *within* the analytic situation itself, regardless of the analyst's or the analysand's interest in spirituality. In the following pages, I will show that not only are analysts today more open to seeing psychoanalysis as a tool to support and enhance the spiritual experience of relevant patients in their lives outside the clinic but psychoanalysis can also be thought of as spiritual *in and of itself.*

The point is not that psychoanalysis has become more spiritual recently, due to the socio-cultural changes described in Chapter 2, but that today, thanks to the new "spiritual tilt," we are able to recognize the spiritual elements that were repressed for decades yet have always been essential in psychoanalytic practice.

DOI: 10.4324/9781003090939-10

The Indian sage Patañjali, author of the *Yoga Sutras*, the most renowned text of yogic practice, defined "practice" as an action done well, intensively, persistently and over a long stretch of time (*Yoga Sutras*, I.14). Patañjali's main commentator, Vyasa, added that a beneficial spiritual practice, one that leads to the stabilization of consciousness, is a daily practice, which is performed out of dedication and knowledge (Sen-Gupta, 2012).

In what follows, I will show how the practice of psychoanalysis could be seen to fit such a definition of spiritual practice. I will start with spiritual elements that can be found in the psychoanalytic situation itself, and then go on to elaborate on spiritual elements in the analytic technique.

Steiner (1976) was perhaps the first to note that psychoanalysis had become a modern substitute for various European spiritual practices such as confession and meditation. Psychoanalysis arose at a moment in history in which techniques of focused introspection and self-interrogation have withered away in Europe, and has thus provided a secular, though heavily mythological, surrogate for these various disciplines.[1]

The sociologist Ernest Gellner (1985) noted that some features of psychoanalysis are shared with intense rituals that are part of various faiths and religions. Like those rituals, the analytic session achieves a "sharp and total *sursis*," he wrote, "a discontinuity with the rest of life, a suspension of its conventions, a heightening of emotion, and yet also presents itself as a precondition of valid comportment in the rest of life" (p. 118). Freud (1926) himself wrote that the function that the analyst performs in relation to the public could be well described by the title "secular pastoral worker" (p. 255).

When the new discipline was first introduced, its secular, scientific elements were emphasized, in order to allow its acceptance. Over the years, this necessity has become less pressing. Prominent analysts such as Eigen (1998b) can now confess: "Therapy is a holy business for me and was so from my first session" (p. 42). To that he added: "I've always felt a sacred element in psychoanalytic psychotherapeutic work, and I've never quite understood the animosity so many analysts have had against the mystical" (p. 191).

Many other writers have elaborated on the claim that psychoanalysis could be "sacred," "holy," "mystical" or generally "spiritual." Rizzuto (2009) wrote that the analytic work is sacred, since one person can enter the inner chambers of another *only* with reverence and respect "owing to the sacredness of this unique territory" (p. 201). Gargiulo (1997) noted that some of the fundamental concerns of traditional Western spirituality can be understood as addressing not only the search for God but the need to experience, as well as to delimit, the autonomous "I." Hence, he argued, "[p]sychoanalysis ... stands in the tradition of Western spirituality in its inquiry into personal meaning and in its efforts to achieve reconciliation" (p. 1).

Analysts also elaborate on spiritual aspects they find in the analytic practice itself. Domash (2009) wrote about an "implicit spirituality" in the analytic situation – expressed in "the meditative quality and deep faith that develops between patient and analyst ... allowing the openness and unconscious freedom that facilitates change" (p. 35). Gargiulo (1997) argued that psychoanalysis offers patients a sort of "salvation," freed from their problematic past. From another perspective, Cernovsky (1988) suggested that psychoanalysis, like Buddhism, offers a healing that can be defined as "liberation" – from being fettered to "misconceptions" and from the suffering caused by being bound in such a way (p. 56).[2]

Such overlaps have prompted analysts to compare the psychoanalytic process with mystical accounts. Gottesfeld (1985) claimed that in both psychoanalysis and mysticism there is a "Transforming Experience," as well as a shift in the way reality is perceived and defined. She described the analytic process in mystic terms: starting with the unpleasant sensation upon the appearance of the first repressed emotions (which she equated with "purgation"), continuing with the analysis of resistance and defences by interpretation ("illumination"), and ending with the termination of analysis leaving the patient feeling harmony and integration ("union").

Along the same lines, Rizzuto (2003) remarked that, just like psychoanalysis, all mystical traditions demand a confrontation of beliefs sustaining identity and manner of living in the world. This task is arduous, she added, "and resisted by well-motivated and established unconscious defenses which must be also transformed" (p. 21).

This point, directly tackled by psychoanalysis, is central to all spiritual traditions. Writing from a Christian perspective, Meissner and Schlauch (2003) noted that both psychoanalysis and spiritual doctrine understand that people involved in a process of searching for understanding regarding the hidden realm of reality will tend – at a certain point – to choose the avenue of least resistance and eventually embrace the illusion they have reached their goal.

Succumbing to this illusion is perhaps the greatest danger that spiritual practitioners, as well as psychoanalysts deal with. Resistance to the analytic process characterizes all phases of it, and, as the analysis proceeds, the resistance frequently becomes stronger. The well-known clinical phenomenon of negative therapeutic reaction concerns the particularly powerful resistance that arises just as there is a move towards new integration. Analysis could thus be seen, wrote Symington (1994), as "an ongoing battle against resistant aspects of the personality," which, he added, "bear[s] all the notes of the spiritual struggle described by mystics both in Western and Eastern religious cultures" (p. 130).

Another spiritual "struggle" is to transform actions that are destructive (or "bad") into actions that are constructive (or "good"). Devoting oneself to bringing about this transformation *is the essence of being spiritual*. Symington (1994) added: "The person who decides to be psychoanalyzed, who struggles with omnipotence and envy and has this as an important aim in his life, is also spiritual" (p. 182).

Finally, if we look at the basic questions spiritual traditions have confronted over the centuries, we will find them very similar to questions that are often tackled in analysis. These basic questions are – How should one live? How is a human being to find fulfilment and satisfaction in his or her life? What is the right path for any one person? Psychoanalysts have a definite answer to such questions, wrote Symington (2004): "We believe ... that to blind ourselves to the truth, to deceive ourselves about the way we behave, leads to unhappiness, ill health, and misery" (p. 162). However, more important than psychoanalysis' view of the world is the place it provides for analysands to find their own answers. In this sense, Gargiulo (1997) wrote, psychoanalysts are "midwives of meaning," who can be seen as

> heirs to Western spiritual traditions. That is, at their best they are Virgilian guides to wandering Dantes, ferreting out what is true from what is no longer true, what is real from what is no longer real, and what is realizable from what is no longer so.
>
> (p. 2)

So far, I discussed spiritual elements in the analytic situation. I will now turn to examine spiritual elements in the psychoanalytic technique.

Besides being a general theory of the mind and "an irreplaceable instrument of scientific research" (Freud, 1917, p. 255), psychoanalysis is basically *a practice*. It is conducted regularly, persistently, and over a long stretch of time; and is supposed to be performed in a certain way, which demands effort, experience and expertise. Beyond the ways analysis affects the analysand and the analyst in a spiritual way, the psychoanalytic technique itself could be seen to be similar in various ways to techniques used in practices commonly referred to as "spiritual."

The psychoanalytic technique "is a very simple one," wrote Freud (1912): "It consists simply in not directing one's notice to anything in particular and in maintaining the same 'evenly-suspended attention' ... in the face of all that one hears" (pp. 111–112). Bion (1970) recommended the analyst "impose on himself a positive discipline of eschewing memory and desire" (p. 31) – including the desire to cure. There is quite a striking similarity between these recommended analytic states-of-mind and the consciousness-state of "bare attention" that Eastern meditation techniques aim for. Maintaining a suspended attention and being with no memory (reflecting the past), nor desire (anticipating a future), leaves one wholly present, as perhaps all spiritual disciplines encourage.[3]

The Indian spiritual teacher Sri Nisargadatta Maharaj (1973) explained: "If you could only keep quiet, *clear of memories and expectations*, you would be able to discern the beautiful pattern of events" (p. 237; emphasis mine). To this he added, again, almost in the same terminology Bion used:

> The window is the absence of the wall and it gives air and light because it is empty. Be empty of all mental content, of all imagination and effort, and the very absence of obstacles will cause reality to rush in. If you really want to help a person, keep away. If you are emotionally committed to helping, you will fail to help.
>
> (p. 249)

Kurtz (1989) referred to a similar quality of mind, known in Japanese Zen as "fūryū" – a term meaning "inspired gesture," an unexpected, free movement, an ability to flow in attunement with the natural world "mindlessly" without being "I-dominated" (pp. 241–243). The ability of the analyst to act spontaneously in this way, he wrote, can be highly therapeutic.[4]

Simmonds (2004) interviewed therapists who use spiritual methods. They said that their spiritual practices were beneficial in aiding them to, at times, put theory aside and achieve such "quality of mind" as described by Bion and others. The participants in the research were in agreement that this quality is an important part of the analytic process, and that, if carried out as recommended, there could be "virtually a meditative process involved" (p. 963).

A parallel demand of presence is placed upon the analysand. According to the "fundamental rule of analysis," that of free associations, the patient is "to put himself into a state of quiet, unreflecting self-observation, and to report to us whatever internal observations he is able to make" (Freud, 1917, p. 328). Again, the resemblance to Eastern meditation is striking. Sri Nisargadatta Maharaj (1973) instructed:

> We know the outer world of sensations and actions, but of our inner world of thoughts and feelings we know very little. The primary purpose of meditation is to become conscious of, and familiar with, our inner life. The ultimate purpose is to reach the source of life and consciousness.
>
> (p. 12)

This similarity was noticed as early as 1924 by Joseph Thompson (writing under the pseudonym Joe Tom Sun), who reflected that morbid emotions are not cured by merely teaching patients their aetiology. The cure, he wrote, "[is] brought about by analysis (vijja, wisdom) which is characterized by instruction and the deepest of meditation, i.e., free association" (p. 43).[5] More recently, Stone (2005) noted that the necessity of self-abandonment in free association, needed to "crack up" the ego and experience the true self, is similar to the process and goal of Buddhist meditation. Lawner (2001) claimed that, like meditation, the free association method, by familiarizing one with her experiential life, fosters a more richly articulated involvement with oneself and one's environment, thus enhancing the capacity "to experience remarkable aspects of one's 'everyday' world" (p. 538).

Being present is not a simple task. In Buddhist insight meditation, it is not the tool but rather the goal. After persistent practice, one might be able to remain focused and aware of what happens moment-by-moment in the ever-changing mind-stream for widening stretches of time. Similarly, as Ferenczi noted, the patient is not cured *by* free associations, but is cured when he or she can freely associate (Phillips, 1998).

The meditative aspect of psychoanalysis has another important aspect. Freud and many of his followers pointed out difficulties in staying with emotional life. It is just very hard to stay with feelings for long. As Eigen (2012) wrote: "We shunt, displace, symbolize, evacuate, substitute, reverse, turn emotional sensations or inklings or premonitions into something else. It is very difficult to stay with experiencing as such" (p. 77). Here another spiritual feature of the analytic technique comes as a help. Zen master and psychoanalyst Barry Magid (2000) wrote that the analytic meeting, like meditation in Zen Buddhism, trains the person to "stay with, tolerate, and explore thoughts and feelings normally felt to be too painful or frightening to endure" (pp. 514–515).

Beyond the meditative quality of the psychoanalytic technique, writers also refer to it as inspiring ecstasy, although not in its common frenzied connotation. Eigen (1992) even claimed that the ecstatic elements of analytic encounters, though rarely acknowledged, might be of its most crucial components. After all, psychoanalysis invites the person to momentarily stand outside oneself and look at oneself, thus touching ecstasy – literally meaning "standing outside of oneself" (*ex stasis*).

Some analysts might not be glad at the thought that what they do, day-in and day-out, dabbles in ecstasy. However, most patients, if not actually saying so, present themselves for psychoanalysis out of a desire for such an experience. As Langan (2003) wrote, "[they] come out of a desire to step outside ways of being that have themselves become straitjackets" (p. 139).

One last psychoanalytic element of technique which resonates spiritual practices is to do with psychoanalysis' intriguing combination of a great ambition, evidenced by the claim to be able to achieve fundamental and stable changes in patients' lives and personalities (see e.g. Freud, 1923; Wallerstein, 1965), with a professed technique of having no goal in mind.

Freud (1912) wrote: "the most successful cases are those in which one proceeds, as it were, without any purpose in view, allows oneself to be taken by surprise by any new turn in them, and always meets them with an open mind, free from any presuppositions" (p. 114). Bion (1970) wrote even more specifically that "the analyst should not permit himself to harbour desires, even the desire to cure, since to do so is inimical to psycho-analytical development. Development itself is not an object that can be 'desired'" (p. 79). And Bollas (1995) stated: "In order to possess a knowledge of who we are, we must be dispossessed of the search; only with this strange dispossession will we get a closer sense of the object we seek" (p. 168).

This strange combination of aspiring to the highest goal while using a technique of goallessness, or "searchlessness," can be found in many spiritual traditions. Mitchell (1993) noted the similarity: "According to the Taoists, setting out to find Enlightenment is like pursuing a thief hiding in the forest by banging loudly on a drum. Setting out to find one's true self or trying to hold onto one's true self entails similar problems" (p. 149). The apparent contradiction between the inevitability of analysts trying to achieve something with their patients and the repeated technical warnings against this, wrote Barnett (2008), is "akin to Zen training" (p. 877).

Indeed, the renowned Zen Buddhist teacher Shunryu Suzuki (1970) spoke of "no gaining idea," as the "right" attitude for Zen practice if one is to achieve mastery in it. By this, he meant having "no particular purpose or goal" (p. 75). Suzuki's advice to the meditator could have been given almost word-by-word by an analyst following Freud's or Bion's advice. Suzuki (1970) said:

> So long as you have some particular goal in your practice, that practice will not help you completely. It may help as long as you are directed toward that goal, but when you resume your everyday life, it will not work.
> (p. 75)

According to Cooper (2002), the relevance of the concept of "no gaining idea" to clinical experience centres on the multi-determined role that problems and goals have in therapy, as they can serve both as points of contact and as buffers between therapist and patient. He wrote: "The notion of no gaining idea prevents the analyst from getting embedded and lost in the content or to take it too literally and lose sight of the many currents that can evolve between two human beings in a consultation room" (p. 109).

After giving his "no memory, no desire" dictum, Bion (1970) wondered "what state of mind is welcome if desires and memories are not." The term he found to "express approximately" what he meant was "faith" – "faith that there is an ultimate reality and truth" (p. 31).

To sum things up, reading the writings of spiritually sensitive analysts, we can see that psychoanalysis is described as a practice that has sacred elements, a practice that evokes a meditative presence, dabbles in ecstasy, is done ideally in a faith-full state of mind, deals with the most profound questions of life, aims at the highest of goals while using a technique of goallessness, creates a shift in the way reality is perceived, increases compassion and care and offers a form of salvation or liberation. As it is supposed to be done well, intensively, persistently and over a long stretch of time, psychoanalysis can be regarded as a spiritual practice.

This vision is also relevant to less demanding, dynamically-oriented therapies. It is not the frequency that counts, even though, as with any spiritual practice, spending more hours on the cushion or mattress (or couch), usually helps. The Tibetans encourage spending a period of three years and one and a half months in retreat (*sum chok sum*), though it does not mean that meditating less than that is not "spiritual." Enlightenment, it is asserted, is not a distant goal achieved after countless hours of meditation – it is here, in every minute. There is nothing to achieve, nothing to aspire to, wrote Genoud (2006), "[a]ttainment and true freedom are as irreconcilable as a crow and an owl" (p. 6). We don't sit to become Buddhas, said Zen master Suzuki (1970), we sit because this is what Buddhas do, this is how we express our "Buddhaness."

In therapy, Eigen (2004) emphasized what he termed "the analytic experience," which he claimed does not depend or necessarily correlate with "externals," such as frequency or use of a couch (see also Bion, 1965, p. 148). This *experience* can occasionally be reached in a single meeting (e.g. Renik, 2001), and – on the other hand – a process of analyst meeting with a patient five times a week "can continue for twenty years without an analysis happening" (Symington, 2012, p. 406).

The "analytic experience" also does not depend on patient and therapist having any spiritual motivation or interest. When both have such an interest, they can actively use analysis to promote specific spiritual goals of the patient. When both are not interested in spirituality, they may perfectly well focus on any of the other three dimensions of psychoanalysis Freud (1926) mentioned – yet even in this case there will be a flavour of spirituality to the process, if only in the meditative aspects of the technique, in the attempt to step outside ways of being that have become restricting or in the striving to improve relations with oneself and others, generating more compassion, care and love.

The same is true with the other dimensions of analysis. Even if analyst and patient, for instance, are not interested in the scientific aspect of psychoanalysis as a tool for investigating the mind, it will be there. In other cases, perhaps such as in training-analysis, the theoretical or scientific aspects might be prominent, yet therapeutic work will nevertheless take place.[6]

The therapeutic dimension, which is usually the central one for most analysts (and of course patients), is particularly intertwined with the spiritual. Spiritual practice is not something egotistic, done only to enhance the seeker's life. Various traditions encourage periods of practicing in solitude, but the ultimate goal is always to be genuinely involved with others. In the well-known *Jūgyū* (*Ten Bulls*) poems and sketches of Japanese Zen, after catching, taming, and transcending the bull (the mind), the spiritual seeker, in the tenth and highest stage of the Path, returns to the marketplace (Suzuki, 1934).

The experience of mystical union is not the end of the path. After that, the mystic is to return to the world, to share what she learned. This is the last, and highest, stage of the journey. As Teresa of Ávila said: "If anyone told me that after reaching this state of union he had enjoyed continued rest and joy, I should say that he had not reached it at all" (quoted in Duerlinger, 1984, p. 68).

This is perhaps the most spiritual element of psychoanalysis, always neglected since it is so obvious. Psychoanalysis is a method to *help other people* live better, fuller, more authentic and meaningful lives, which is – after all – the goal of all spiritual traditions.

This brings us to one more element uniting all spiritual paths. The extent of help given to the neighbour – the other – is dependent on the love for him or her the spiritual person can cultivate. The purer the love, the greater the help. How psychoanalysis allows for a pure kind of love – the acme of all spiritual traditions – to arise in the hearts of its practitioners, will be described in detail in the next chapter.

Notes

1. From the 14th to the early 18th century, Steiner (1976) noted, a certain form of meditation – in which the worshipper observed him- or herself, and which is quite similar to psychoanalysis – was very popular in Europe. Journals, texts of meditation and manuals of exercises of self-examination and penitence of that period point to a wealth and discipline of unspoken discourse that has been forgotten since then. Believers of that period, wrote Steiner, spent hours in articulate meditation on God and the self. Thus, psychoanalysis revived an ancient Western practice, which had disappeared, "[giving] institutional licence [*sic.*] to the outward articulation of what had formerly been the preserve of internal speech" (p. 257).
2. Analysts influenced by Buddhism stress not just the ways psychoanalysis is similar to Buddhism, but also the opposite. Young-Eisendrath (2008) showed that the 13th-century Japanese Zen teacher Dogen has a complex theory of "a relational self." Finn (2003) wrote that Buddhist writings nearly a thousand years old contain notions of analytic ideas such as Oedipal dynamics, transitional space, and transference. Finally, Epstein (1995) claimed

that Buddha himself "may well have been the original psychoanalyst," or at least the first to use an analytic inquiry that Freud later systematized and developed (p. 9).
3. Evidence to this can be found in titles of spiritual bestsellers such as *The Power of Now* (Tolle, 1997) or *Be Here Now* (Ram Das, 1971). The Hebrew name of God also alludes to this idea – Yahweh (יהוה) means, quite literally, 'always becoming present.'
4. As an example, Kurtz (1989) described a frustrating treatment with an artist who had difficulties in her personal and professional life. After weeks of exasperating work, something in him snapped: "A noise came out of me – a sound that felt, from the inside, like a deep twanging drone, growing louder and louder without losing its snarl and roll. The noise filled me until I was aware of nothing else." When the sound subsided, therapist and patient "stared at one another, silenced and dumbfounded. After a while, a smile flickered on her face. Soon we were both grinning, then laughing like kids with the giggles. The session ended without comment" (p. 243). Two things happened afterward, which Kurtz understood as outcomes of that session: The woman found a partner with whom she created a loving relationship, for the first time in her life; and her works of art became "luminous" and less strange. In fact, she became a highly successful artist.
5. Freud was probably not aware of Buddhist meditation techniques when he devised the free association method, but the method's origin, Bakan (1958) postulated, could lie in the meditation techniques of Jewish mysticism.
6. It is hard to believe this today, but in the heyday of scientifically-oriented Ego psychology, many deemed the therapeutic dimension of psychoanalysis superfluous. Eissler (1965), for example, wrote that the analytic situation is one of "pure research" (p. 68) and that the "therapeutic coloring that pervades the psychoanalytic situation... does not reflect the essentials of the psychoanalytic process" (p. 72). Quite similarly, Kubie (1959) wrote "I want to state unequivocally my regret that from the very outset psychoanalysis became a therapeutic instrument, instead of having had the benefit of starting out as an instrument for and as an object of basic research in the technique of microscopic psychological investigation, unbiased by therapeutic needs, demands, and urgencies" (pp. 58–59).

Chapter 7

A love through cure
The spirit of analytic relationship

The central issue of spiritual traditions is not sacrifices or rituals, but the way a person behaves towards others. The main message of Buddha and Jesus, before they were "institutionalized," was to develop an attitude of compassion towards fellow human beings. Yet this is not an easy task. A central part of the spiritual process includes purifying motivation, through increased awareness – otherwise we want to do good, but cause harm.

Here is where the greatest contribution of psychoanalysis as a spiritual practice may be located. The daily expressions of hostility and selfishness, the hurts we cause, are to a large extent emotional and unconscious – but religions usually don't talk about it. That is why someone can be a devout Christian, Muslim, Hindu or Jew, give charity, pray, perform all precepts but "[h]is unconscious activity may be extremely destructive" (Symington, 1994, p. 146). His family and friends may see it but he won't.

One of the central issues that is encountered clinically is that of narcissism, the state of mind where the id has taken its ego as a love object. Such a state precludes compassion and care for others. All spiritual traditions could be seen as trying to release the person from this basic human condition. Psychoanalysis' focus on the unconscious, as well as its interpersonal setting, can greatly enhance the

DOI: 10.4324/9781003090939-11

process of becoming a more aware and compassionate person.

The main arena for spiritual struggle nowadays, claimed Symington (1994), is not in the desert or on a remote mountaintop, but in the interpersonal context. This is where people in the West often face the biggest challenges to their compassion and equanimity. And the more intimate the relationship, the harder it gets. As Leonard Cohen told Rebecca De Mornay, his fiancé at the time:

> Look, here's what I know: marriage is the hardest spiritual practice in the world. People wonder how anybody can sit on Mount Baldy for hours on end, weeks, months, even, but it's nothing compared to marriage. If you're really there, really present, for marriage, it's self-reflection, twenty-four/seven. In other words, who you are is reflected back to you in the mirror of your marriage partner, daily, minute by minute, hour by hour. Who can take that?
> (Quoted in Simmons, 2012, p. 406)

In the context of intimate relationships, compassion and care are usually only part of the picture. Love encompasses compassion and care, but can go beyond these.

This is true not only in the field of romance. Love has always been *the* supreme virtue of spiritual traditions. "Love, in its essence, *is* spiritual fire," claimed theologian and mystic Emanuel Swedenborg (1771, p. 56). And St John declared: "God is love, and he who abides in love abides in God, and God in him" (1 John 4:16, New King James Version). That "God is love," commented Józef Tischner, is *the only* basic dogma of Christianity, "the dogma of dogmas, from which all formulas shoot up like branches from a trunk" (quoted in Bielawka, 2009, p. 154).

Originally, the source and the object of the highest form of love was God. Over the centuries, the object changed to our fellow humans, and the source of love shifted from God to the inner heart, making the wholly, truly loving person into an embodiment of divinity (May, 2011).

Of course, loving intensely and purely is not easy. Such love requires maximal awareness and minimal attachment to ego. Psychoanalysis seems to be directed exactly there, as can be evidenced by a close inspection of the psychoanalytic setting itself. This is what the current chapter will attempt to do.

The analytic setting may be Freud's most significant contribution, argued Modell (1988), though "paradoxically" one to which he paid scant attention (p. 583). Khan (1972) too claimed that

> [t]he greatest invention of Freud will always be the invention of this unique human situation where a person can explore the meaning and experiential realities of his life, through a relationship with another, and yet not be intruded upon or manipulated in any way that is not true to his own self and values.
>
> (p. 127)

The analytic frame, I will show here, has formed and evolved, mostly unconsciously, to allow and even induce the appearance of loving feelings and behaviours. This is true for the analysand, of course, but even more importantly for the analyst.

The analytic setting is associated basically with the establishment and maintenance of the physical setting of the clinic and with the psychoanalytic contract (Freud, 1913; Winnicott, 1956; Bleger, 1967). Some analysts also mention the analytic attitude as part of the setting, perhaps even the most important part (Carpelan, 1981). This attitude is defined by a series of values that are not commonplace in everyday life, such as compassion, care, fairness and truthfulness (Tubert-Oklander, 2008).

Another vital element of the psychoanalytic setting is its extraordinary interpersonal arrangement, which is anchored by two complementary ways of relating: free-association and analytic neutrality (Adler & Bachant, 1996). Together, these two structure an interaction that takes a specific shape at any moment of the treatment as a co-construction of the analyst and analysand (Hernández-Tubert, 2008).

The setting also includes clear boundaries. These guarantee the safety of both participants by channelling and absorbing the powerful psychological forces released by the analytic process.

Collectively, the structural elements of the analytic situation create a space where two people have the opportunity to listen to and to partake in their own and in each other's thoughts and feelings and the movements of the unconscious. Rather than saying that the establishment of the setting reproduces an object relation, Green (1975) found it "more appropriate to say that it is this which *allows* the birth and development of an object relation" (p. 11; emphasis added). This new object relation, born in a context of holding, containing, and understanding in a spirit of compassion and care, is a relationship which is loving in essence, as I will go on to show.

Love as the epitome of a worthy, healthy life, has always been a central tenet in analytic theory and practice. As Fromm (1950) wrote: "Analytic therapy is essentially an attempt to help the patient gain or regain his capacity for love" (p. 87). Concluding his classic, *Theory of Psychoanalytic Technique*, Menninger (1958), wrote that the outcome of a successful analysis is a patient who has learned to live, that is – to love and to be loved. Within the philosophy of psychoanalysis, Menninger continued, it is implicit that "love is the greatest thing in the world" (pp. 178–179). Half a century later, to take an incidental example, Fosshage (2007) wrote similarly that "[f]undamental experiences of love – that is, to love and to be loved – are central in development and maintenance of vitalized self-experience" (p. 330).

Of these two vital human growth experiences, to love and to be loved, analysts have usually focused on the first as the aim of treatment. This line of practice originated in Freud's famous remark in his 1906 letter to Jung, that psychoanalysis is a healing effected through love ("eigentlich eine Heilung durch Liebe"), repeated three years later in a letter to Eitingon, where Freud wrote, "the secret of therapy is to cure through love" (quoted in Falzeder, 1994, p. 310).

What he had in mind, Freud made clear, was the patient's love towards the analyst, aroused in the transference. "The process of cure is accomplished in a relapse into love … Every psycho-analytic treatment is an attempt at liberating repressed love which has found a meagre outlet in the compromise of a symptom" (Freud, 1907, pp. 89–90).

This "liberation" is actively evoked by the analyst and by the "medical situation" (Freud, 1915, p. 162). Celenza (2007) stressed "the seductiveness" of this situation: the patient falling in love, she wrote, "[is] structured into the setting. This fact is definitional and must be accepted as a given" (p. 298). The setting models the analyst as a constant, caring, empathic, understanding, powerful presence, which naturally "seduces" the patient to develop loving feelings towards him or her.

Managing to seduce this kind of "curative" love has a crucial condition. Natterson (2003) stressed that the fostering of love in the patient "is possible only in a mutually loving relationship" (p. 514). The first step in the therapeutic love affair is often to be taken by the analyst, as for many patients feeling the therapist's genuine love is a precondition to them being able to discover their own capacities to love (Gerrard, 2005).

Yet Freud had very little to say of the analyst's love for the patient. In his observations on transference love Freud (1915) only reminded of "the universally accepted standards of morality" and insisted "that the analyst must never under any circumstances accept or return the tender feelings that are offered him" (p. 163). In a letter to Eitingon, Freud advised his friend "to develop the thick skin we need ... to dominate 'countertransference,' which is after all a permanent problem for us" (quoted in Falzeder, 1994, p. 310). To Marie Bonaparte he wrote in the clearest words: "One must never love one's patients. Whenever I thought I did, the analysis suffered terribly from it. One ought to remain completely cool" (quoted in Weinstein, 1986, p. 104).

In the many decades that passed, this warning did not disappear from analysts' minds. Long after the "relational turn" in psychoanalysis, theoretical writings that refer to the role of analytic love are still rare to find (Cohen, 2006). The same is true with case presentations Erotic or aggressive countertransference are indeed widely conferred the status of therapeutic agents, Shaw (2003) observed, and natural warmth, openness and expressiveness are no longer considered anti-analytic, "[y]et case presentations where feelings of tenderness, affection, and love for an analysand are openly expressed are often greeted with suspicion" (p. 253).

The main objection is that if the analyst has loving feelings for a patient, these will make it very difficult to preserve the analytic posture of neutrality (Coen, 1994). In addition, loving analysts are often accused of "acting out" their narcissistic need to cure (Shaw, 2003).

Yet this warned-of, seemingly non-analytic feeling – love – is exactly where the setting leads the therapist. And for good reasons. Uncomfortable as it might be for some analysts, loving the patient is being increasingly recognized as crucial for therapeutic success.

The first to openly state so was Ferenczi (1932/1988), who saw "an all conquering love" for *each and every patient* as a necessary condition for a curative process to take place. "[N]o analysis can succeed if we do not succeed in really loving the patient," he claimed (pp. 129–130).

This position was highly criticized at the time. Classical, "one-person" psychoanalysis emphasized understanding patients and discovering the truth about their past and not the relationship formed with them (Lev, 2016). Slowly, though, other voices emerged. Segal (1962), for one, wrote that "a good therapeutic setting must include unconscious love in the analyst for the patient" (p. 232).

More recently, claims such as "[l]ove is the glue that cements the analytic work" (Weinstein, 2007, p. 306) or "analytic love [is] a core mechanism of therapeutic action" (Wolson, 2011, p. 184) have become more mainstream. The patient's love for the analyst is not a *sine qua non* of the treatment, wrote Fink (2015), certainly not in its initial stages, but "if the analyst cannot find at least something to love in a particular analysand, trouble will ineluctably ensue and the analyst would do better to refer the analysand to a trusted fellow practitioner" (p. 82).

Thorne (2011) wrote that his experience has convinced him that it is essential for him to love his clients if genuine healing is to occur. He added that "the deeper the wound or the greater the deficiency, the more likely it is that I shall have to extend myself in love to a degree which is costly in effort and commitment" (p. 164).

The point, many analysts agree, is that in order to be able to change, many people need to feel loved. Fairbairn (1952) said that the greatest need of a child is to obtain conclusive assurance of two things: That he is genuinely loved as a person by his parents, and that his parents genuinely accept his love. Frustration of this twofold desire, Fairbairn went on, "is *the greatest trauma* that a child can experience" (p. 39; emphasis added). Ferenczi's idea was that in order to undo this common, yet "greatest" of traumas, the analyst must be able to genuinely love the patient.

In a more recent description of this line of thinking, Gerrard (2005) suggested that most of the people who approach therapy feel themselves unlovable at some very deep level, and hence unless there are felt moments of love for the patient by the therapist, the patient will not able to develop fully. She concluded: "I think it is only when a patient can arouse our deepest loving feelings (not empathy) that we can really hope for a truly positive outcome from our work" (p. 27).

Such loving feelings convey to patients a deep and full acceptance of who they are, which is by itself therapeutic. The American psychoanalyst Thomas Malone (1976) claimed the following to be "the most significant discovery" he has come to in thirty years of practice:

> Before you can help anyone be different, you have to accept them as they are. ... Unless this occurs, nothing eventuates in the therapy. This means loving – enjoying – being with them as they are, without any insistence they have to be different for you to love them.
>
> (quoted in Field, 1999, p. 95)

Such love is to be thought of not just in terms of transference and countertransference. Of course, there could be a love which is transferential but the form of love under discussion is not one which necessarily constitutes the reconstruction of some previous relationship (Cohen, 2006). It is mostly genuine, spontaneous expressions of love performed by the analyst that are powerful and potentially transformative (Stern, 2011).

Such a powerful, genuine emotion on the analyst's side, was perhaps most lucidly described by Harold Searles (1959). He wrote:

I have found, time after time, that in the course of the work with every one of my patients who has progressed to, or very far toward, a thoroughgoing analytic cure, I have experienced romantic and erotic desires to marry, and fantasies of being married to, the patient. Such fantasies and emotions have appeared in me usually relatively late in the course of treatment, have been present not briefly but usually for a number of months.

(p. 180)

Love toward the patient is crucial for the therapeutic process, many analysts agree. Still, feeling "romantic and erotic desires," in the way described by Searles, can also be complicated and dangerous. First, one can argue, a loving, benevolent position might unconsciously oppose and preclude some patients' need to experience the analyst, in the safety of the transference relationship, as a "bad" or even "terrible" object that does harm (Mitrani, 2001; Charles, 2017).

Yet letting a loved patient experience oneself as terrible *is in itself*, in certain cases, an expression of analytic love. Only a loving attitude could allow an analyst to take on herself unpleasant roles and attitudes while facing the patient, if that is what is needed for the patient's growth and health. Otherwise it is not loving the other, but oneself.

Another objection raised against the analyst loving the patient is that the analyst may lose her freedom when not guarded by the principles of abstinence and neutrality (e.g. Freud, 1915). Of course, if unanalysed by the therapist, such loving feelings could hamper the analytic process. Yet sticking fiercely to the principles of abstinence and neutrality can be no less problematic (Hoffman, 2009). As Charles (2017) wrote, "we are always up against the line between too much thinking and too much feeling"

(p. 187). Both extremes can be problematic, not just the "too much feeling" one.

In the most extreme cases of unanalysed countertransference, the analyst may act as a perpetrator due to confusion with respect to the concept of love (Ferenczi, 1934/1949). Chessick (1997) distinguished malignant "eroticized" countertransference, which often leads to sexual enactment, from "erotic" countertransference, which is therapeutic once properly analysed and understood (e.g. Davies, 1994). Of course, eroticized countertransference has nothing to do with actual love *for the patient*.

Love, we must keep in mind, can appear in various forms, in everyday life as well as in the clinic. Just as there are growth-promoting, mutually enhancing forms of love, in life and in the clinic, so there are also perverse, sadomasochistic "loving" that arise between romantic partners as well as between patient and therapist (Novick & Novick, 2000).

Love's presence could be problematic, but so can be its lack. Analytic literature is rife with descriptions of so-called love, gone awry. Spiritually sensitive psychoanalysis adds to that a fuller appreciation of the growth-promoting forms of analytic love.

Coltart (1992) spoke of love in general as a mystery, impossible to capture by the language of psychological theory. Analytic love is perhaps even more difficult to define. This love resembles at times parental love, at others fraternal love, charitable love, friendly love, erotic love and so forth, yet it is "not simply or actually any of those ... It is a thing unto itself" (Shaw, 2003, p. 268). Nacht (1962) wrote that the analyst's inner attitude "should be impregnated with love for his patient," and added that "[i]t is a kind of openness that one can understand only if he has already experienced it himself with his patients in the analytic relationship" (p. 233). This is a love unlike any other, Nacht continued, "it is a kind of love in which [one] is not personally concerned, although it *is* a deep feeling" (p. 233).

This combination of deep feeling with a degree of detachment mandated by the analyst's role, could seem to be contradictory, yet is in fact perhaps the strongest defining characteristic of analytic love. This love is sublimated and at the same time passionate; modulated while being libidinal (Ferenczi, 1932/1988).

Another defining element of therapeutic love is that, in essence, it is not equal nor mutual in the ordinary sense, although the analyst and patient may both strongly love each other (Hoffer, 1993; Hoffman, 1993). It is the analyst alone who is completely committed to the patient's safety, and to the attentive attempt of trying to understand the patient and to help him or her understand themselves (Frank, 1987; Shaw, 2003). Analytic love is thus characterized by an effort "to make sure that whatever we are feeling, and whatever we consciously do to act on these feelings, are, to the best of our ability, truly in the interests of the patient and his or her analytic growth" (Stern, 2011, p. 497). This means the analyst's love must be maximally conscious, aware, reflective.

The non-equality also means, as Fink (2015) stressed, that "the analyst must love without wanting to be loved in return" (p. 78). The loving analyst refuses to adopt the position of the beloved in the analytic setting.

But is this love "real"? At some level on any patient's mind, implicitly or explicitly, this question rises (Nussbaum, 2005). Hoffer (1993) insisted that "the positive feelings between analyst and analysand are real, not imitations" (p. 355). Similarly, Gerrard (2005) described "moments, not of compassion, pity or empathy, but of an unspoken rush of feeling of 'I really love you' for a patient" (p. 27).

As with the paradox of the analyst's love being both passionate *and* self-controlled, a similar "both," instead of "either or" solution could be given to the question of the realness of the analyst's love. Stern (2011) suggested that the analyst's feelings toward the patient are always both real and counter transferential, and it is crucial to the patient that they be *both* – that the paradox be maintained and even held as sacred. Stern wrote:

> The patient needs the analyst to *really* care about or love him or her. Nothing less can transform the patient's real feelings of self-loathing and unloveability. However, he or she also needs the analyst always to "remember" that these real feelings are occurring within the unique context of an analytic relationship – a relationship with certain purposes, a certain role structure, and a unique frame within which conscious and unconscious experience are "invited" into a co-creative dialogue.
>
> (p. 496)

Such a paradoxical love is not easy to deliver. How do analysts stand up to this high therapeutic as well as spiritual standard of truly, deeply loving while always keeping in mind the context of this love and its purpose? We have the aid of our clinical experience and knowledge, and beyond these – we have the significant support of the analytic setting itself.

The analytic situation is founded upon a search for truth – the truth of the analysand's psychic reality (Freud, 1937). According to Steingart (1995), being devoted to uncovering this truth develops in the analyst an "extraordinary" (p. 111) love towards the patient's psychic reality. The analyst possesses, Steingart continued,

> a real, (relatively) mature love for the analysand's mind and all that the analysand produces with his or her mind. It matters not whether what the analysand

produces with his or her mind is expressive, resistant, creative, perverse, adaptive, maladjusted, loving, hateful, or whatever – all are equally loved by the analyst because they are ways in which the analysand produces his or her psychic reality with his or her mind.

(pp. 118–119)

This deep interest is in a way similar to Winnicott's (1956) "primary maternal preoccupation." Parents can usually develop this attitude thanks to biological and social conditioning. In therapy, the setting is what allows this stance to arise. Freud thus created, suggested Steingart (1995), "a new type of love relationship" (p. 112).

One might argue that a position of seeking truth and understanding about someone is not equivalent to "loving" that person. Loewald's (1970) words could serve as an answer: "It is impossible to love the truth of psychic reality, to be moved by this truth as Freud was in his life work, and not to love and care for the object whose truth we want to discover" (p. 297).

The setting induces a profound, loving interest in our patients' psyche, which further leads to a unique, intense knowledge and understanding of our patients' personality and psychic life. This serves to intensify that love even more. Freud (1910) commented: "in truth great love springs from great knowledge of the beloved object" (p. 74). Such "great knowledge" is exactly what the analytic setting allows us. Friedman (2005) even claimed that the heightened knowledge achieved in analysis "might even be *the most intense knowledge possible of a singular existence*" (p. 362, emphasis added).[1]

The analytic attitude, as mentioned, is in itself an essential feature of the setting. This attitude is one in which the analyst maintains a constant and reliable presence, directed to the patient's wellbeing while keeping his or her our own needs from intruding. Such a position, wrote

Modell (1988), "[is] analogous, but not at all identical, to a mother-child relationship, so that analysands may experience being held by the analytic setting" (p. 582). The analyst's dedication to the growth and to the safety of the analysand, wrote Shaw (2003), "is in essence an act of love" (p. 269).

Being dedicated to such a degree, hour after hour, day after day, week after week, could be seen to demand super-human capacities. Most people are not able to perform in such a way in daily life, not even in close relationships. This is what spiritual practitioners from various traditions practice on for long periods, sometimes for their entire life. How can so many analysts manage to pull it together?

This too could be seen to be a consequence of the analytic meeting's structure. Some analysts claim that the analytic situation brings out a "second self," which is consistently benevolent, empathic, accepting and loving (Schafer, 1983).

Outside the clinic our relationships are "simply human," wrote Kernberg (1994, p. 1147). We become defensive when criticized, we sometimes avoid intimacy, and can get irritated, even quite easily. Yet in the analytic situation, we can regularly function, without too much difficulty, at a level of empathy rarely met in ordinary life.

The second self is not an illusion or a mask, but very real (Steingart, 1995). The setting does not make us different from who we actually are. In fact, it demands we become ourselves as much as possible. The second self should perhaps be called the first, or as the Zen Koan goes, "the original" (face) (Red Pine, 2008). Under our analytic hat, we are not only highly interested in the patient's psyche, but are also, at least ideally, singularly attuned to our own. This, in turn, makes us love ourselves in this situation and then the patient, even more. When one is deeply oneself in the presence of another, one becomes authentic and loving, one becomes, as Mendelsohn (2007) wrote, "accepting and trusting of whatever emerges" (p. 226).

The acceptance and trust are supported by the strict and agreed upon boundaries of the situation, which guarantee the safety of both participants. Privacy and confidentiality reign in the clinic, and so it can contain all kinds of intense or threatening affects that may appear. The clinical setting could thus be seen as "a kind of sanctuary" for emotions (Mendelsohn, 2007, p. 233), which allows patient and analyst to come to know each other deeply and to transform each other.

One more defining feature of the second self is that it involves a unique point-of-view, from which every weakness, every "flaw" the patient shows – is seen not as an expression of evilness, stupidity or indifference, as they would perhaps be seen if observed from the point of view of the "first," everyday self, but as an expression of the pain of non-love. Each scar, from this perspective, renders the face with beauty.

The therapeutic setting creates in us the ability to see goodness and beauty in patients of a whole range of age, appearance, character and pathology. Nothing is more spiritual than that. Searles (1959) wrote that one of his first experiences of profound analytic love, the sort under discussion here, was with a much older hebephrenic woman.

This accepting and affirming point of view enables us to see in our patients something which is true of every person, yet rarely observed. Flynn Campbell (2005) called this the "divine essence" of the patient. She went on unhesitatingly:

> There comes a moment with some patients when I feel like I am seeing them as through the eyes of a loving God. In these moments I am full of a kind of love that comes from something outside of myself, as if I am

briefly possessed by a Godly presence that perceives the human condition in all its heart-wrenching beauty and pain.

(p. 71)

Analysts and analysands struggle daily to remove resistances and obstacles to the familiar kind of love, that of the "love and work" duo. Yet analysis sometimes goes beyond that. In his last poem, Edgar Alan Poe (1849) wrote: "but we loved with a love which is more than love." Field (1999) tried to analytically describe such love, a love that is transcendent. He wrote about "mature relationships," relationships based on the emergence of a flexible, well-functioning ego, which is what therapy usually aims to achieve. The kind of love that characterizes these relationships he called "three-dimensional love."[2] But there is also a "true love," he claimed, which is "*beyond* the three dimensional, beyond Klein's depressive position, beyond Freud's secondary process" (p. 97). This love, according to Field, incorporates, underlies and transcends the ego. He wrote:

> I want to suggest the possibility of a four-dimensional relationship. I have in mind those moments – and they are usually very brief – where two people feel profoundly united with one another yet each retains a singularity [*sic*.] enriched sense of themselves. Because it feels to be of quite a different order from everyday experience, we are inclined to call it an "altered state." But when we are *in* it we realise with a shock of joyful recognition that it is our *true state* and everyday experience is, by comparison, a shrunken form of consciousness.
>
> (p. 97)

Because of its paradoxical nature, four-dimensional love cannot be mentally grasped, rather "we have to let it grasp us" (Field, 1999, p. 97). This is analogous to Bion's (1970) "O," that "can be 'become,' but ... cannot be 'known'" (p. 26), and, according to Field (1999), also "to Einstein's four-dimensional union of space and time, in that it involves the paradoxical *union and separation of self and other*. We are not lost in one another – that would be one-dimensional – but found" (p. 100).[3] According to Field, the four-dimensional might be reached in few ways: "In art, in nature, in prayer, in mystical experience, sometimes in childbirth, and also in the therapeutic encounter" (p. 100).

The union in love that Field talked about brings to mind Plato's (2008 [385–370 BCE]) *Symposium*. The great Greek philosopher wrote there about humankind's greatest aspiration: to find our "other half" and be united with him or her. This merger is the holy grail all humans seek "since far-off time" – "to restore us to our ancient state by trying to make unity out of duality and to heal our human condition" (p. 24).

Such union, Plato warned, "happens rarely" (p. 26). Making it more prevalent is perhaps the greatest achievement ever attributed to the analytic setting. Indeed, according to Eshel (2019), such union is what transpires in analysis: "the deep patient-analyst interconnectedness ... is not one- or two-person psychology, but an emergent two-in-oneness that is fundamentally inseparable into its two participants – an analytic oneness that transcends the duality of patient and analyst, transference and countertransference" (p. 4).

If a certain form of love is the highest spiritual attainment, as mystics from all traditions declare, one can argue that the analytic practice, which encourages, facilitates and even demands the analyst love unconditionally, persistently, intensively, out of dedication and knowledge, *is* spiritual. It is a daily work of love.

Whatever the philosophical disposition of the analyst, whatever his or her theoretical orientation, the analyst's love is essential to the analytic cure – whether he or she embraces the fact, resists it or represses it. Vida (2002) remarked that we cannot even say that the analyst's love "contributes" to analysis, since it is not an option or a conscious choice whether it is there or not. She likened the question whether love contributes to analysis to asking, "does it contribute to the therapeutic action that the analyst draws breath, has a blood pressure, and a pulse?" (p. 437). "We all," wrote Coltart (1991), "have the repeated experience of coming to like, certainly to care for, and probably, if we are deeply open to ourselves and unafraid, to love *each patient* as the analysis unfolds" (p. 449–450; emphasis added).

This is not a simple type of love but one that is highly demanding in the discipline it imposes (Thorne, 2011). The analyst is required to know and understand the patient in a profound way, which is based on, and draws from, the love towards the patient. Feeling loved for who he or she is, truly, with no masks or pretence, the patient can now come to love him or herself, and then love back. With this regained capacity, the patient returns to the world a different person.

Looked at from this perspective, we can add that beyond being a theory, a practice, a language and a method for investigation (Cooper, 1985; Gellner, 1985; Lev, 2017) psychoanalysis is *a relationship* of a very special kind. Steingart (1995) wrote: "The crux of the matter is that Freud created not only a new theory of human nature but, interrelated with that theory, a new type of human relationship" (pp. 108–109). Indeed, Freud (1915) himself was aware that this relationship "is one for which there is no model in real life" (p. 166).

What we are coming to understand is that the essence of this "unmodelled" relationship is that it allows love to arise. This is what many features in the setting in which this relationship takes place actually promote: the protective boundaries create an atmosphere of safety and trust – without which one cannot genuinely love; the topic of the conversation – the human psyche – encourages emotional involvement; the unique combination of passion and neutrality allows intense authenticity and knowledge.

We need to remember that while love might be crucial to most, if not all patients, it is not *all* that is necessary. Theory, knowledge, experience are vital too. "Love is certainly not enough," admitted Gerrard (2005), before adding: "but then again, in my view, neither is interpretation, containment, reverie or any other psychoanalytical activity without the backing of love" (p. 37).

Psychoanalysts have been ambivalent for decades about the role of their own loving feelings: are they necessary, genuine, therapeutic? Is love a problem or a vehicle for change? With the liberating understandings of Spiritually sensitive psychoanalysis regarding love's unique place in the general order of things, as well as in the analytic process, perhaps we have finally come at a time in the development of our profession when we can calmly and wholeheartedly trust our love to our patients – which is where the analytic setting itself leads us for over a century. As Freud (1909) wrote: "a man who doubts his own love may, or rather *must*, doubt every lesser thing" (p. 241).

Notes

1. The patient too has great knowledge of the analyst, even if of a different kind. The patient acquires a deep acquaintance of how the analyst reacts to weakness, sadness, dependence, etc. (e.g., Cooper 2000). The patient's knowledge of the analyst also adds to the analyst's love. Being known leads to love, both ways – for the knower, as well as for the known.
2. According to Field (1999), *one-dimensional* love appears in the first phases of development, as can be seen in very small infants, who exist in a world where there is minimal

differentiation between self and other. *Two-dimensional* love is characterized by perceptions distorted by paranoia or idealization of the people we become involved with (this belongs to Melanie Klein's paranoid-schizoid position). *Three-dimensional* love is adult, reflective, resilient, capable of integrating good and bad (belongs to Klein's depressive position).
3. This is quite similar to Fromm's (1956) famous statement: "Mature love," he wrote, "is union under the condition of preserving one's integrity, one's individuality ... In love the paradox occurs that two beings become one and yet remain two" (p. 19).

Conclusion

Ecstasy and suffering resting in one another: The contribution of spiritually sensitive psychoanalysis

Since the beginning of 21st century one can notice a wave of psychoanalysts discussing and experiencing spirit in an approach very different from the one prevalent in the preceding 100 years of the discipline's history. Simmonds (2006) wrote that this process creates "a sea change" in analytic theory (p. 128) and Sorenson (2004a) declared that for psychoanalysis this "paradigm shift" is as dramatic and far-reaching as was the Copernican revolution for 16th-century astronomy.

Parsons (2007) noticed the irony in that today "certain forms of metapsychology have come to a position closer to Rolland than to Freud" (p. 92). Freud's thought, however, should not be reduced to a reduction of the religious into the pathological. Freud also had curiosity and openness to the mysteries of existence, which he curbed, in order to promote the acceptance of psychoanalysis by the public and by the scientific community of the early 20th century.

For decades, the psychoanalytic establishment held on to this approach, but by the end of that century, the cultural atmosphere became very different. Changes in Western society, which became more open to the religious *Weltanschauung*, and specifically to spiritual ideas, led many psychoanalysts to start investigating avenues that were considered verboten.

The accumulated insights of this endeavour, which was done personally by dozens, even hundreds of analysts, each interested and devoted to both the analytic and the spiritual paths, were not sufficiently discussed so far as a whole. In this book, I tried to do justice to this emerging tradition, which I call spiritually sensitive psychoanalysis.

This new stream of psychoanalytic thought understands spirituality and faith as important and potentially positive elements in the human experience, and not necessarily as evidence for underlying pathology. Spiritually sensitive psychoanalysis helps patients deal with problematic God-representations and with spiritual traps, bypasses and blind spots. In addition, it sets ideals that include encouraging a compassionate moral stance and social responsibility, reducing excessive involvement with the self and even aspiring to mystical experiences of no-self, unity, ecstasy or contact with the numinous. To the existing models of "tragic man," "guilty man" and "dependent man," Spiritually sensitive psychoanalysis offers to add "sacrificing man." In addition to the paranoid-schizoid and depressive positions, it offers a third, "transcendent position." And to the common understandings of the self it contributes a new perspective, from which a stable, isolated and inherent self is seen as an illusion.

At this stage of its development, the young school of thought still has many uncharted areas to explore, and the picture will certainly get fuller and clearer with the years and with more publications like the current one. As it is in many ways antithetic to traditional analytic approaches, it also arises criticisms. In this concluding part of the book, I will try to address a few of them.

Cohen (2003) noted critically that the word "'spirituality' seems to be on everyone's tongue" (p. 269). Even the prestigious Templeton Foundation, she mentioned, was offering grants to design curricula on spirituality for psychiatric residents and to the research of spiritual transformation. Yet, despite the rising popularity of the term, she wrote, "we are not entirely clear about what [it] means" (ibid). The term's vagueness, she continued, leaves it unclear how exactly spirituality could be incorporated into our lives and into our work with patients.

Indeed the realm of the spiritual is obscure. O cannot be *known*, Bion emphasized. Conceptualizations of what exactly is "the spiritual" that psychoanalysis is becoming "sensitive" to, or how is it enhanced in therapy will perhaps never be fully satisfying. In this book I tried to make the term a little clearer, first by attempting a definition of the term (in the Introduction), and by placing the new movement in a context in the history of psychoanalysis (Chapter 1) and in the cultural history of the West in general (Chapter 2). I then elaborated on its contributions to psychoanalytic theory and technique (Chapter 3) and on its implications for the perception of the healthy individual and the life worth living and how these affect the goals of treatment (Chapters 4 and 5). Lastly, I showed how spirituality is in fact embedded in the core of psychoanalysis since its very inception – how the psychoanalytic situation and technique are essentially spiritual (Chapter 6), and how the analytic setting is ingeniously, though unconsciously, designed to induce and enhance the highest spiritual ideal, that of altruistic love (Chapter 7).

Another objection came from Rachel Blass (2004). She claimed the contemporary spiritual/mystical emphasis in psychoanalytic writings on the subjective experience, leads to "blurring of the concern for truth and reality" (p. 630), a concern that is arguably the most central issue to psychoanalysis.

"Truth and reality," however, are not an objective thing, are not "objects." Perhaps the only truth in the deep sense of the word that can be reached, the essence of Truth itself, is subjective, phenomenological. Certainly, this is the case when dealing with the truth of the human psyche.

If this is the state of things, then truth is not something that can be learned, unearthed or known, but only experienced, "be," "become." It is in fact to *this* sense of truth that psychoanalysis has *always* been directed, even if too often it was not aware of doing so.

It might still be claimed that the spiritual aspect contradicts the scientific aspect of psychoanalysis. Such a view understands science in a limited way. Modern-day physics, based on discoveries such as the entanglement of particles beyond space and time, and which has long proved that the observing consciousness influences reality, sounds decidedly "unscientific" in itself. Scientists themselves remind us that physical laws refer not to "nature," but to our *relation* to it (Aronowitz, 1988; Rovelli, 1996). This makes psychoanalysis perfect for the role Freud (1917) designed for it, "an irreplaceable instrument of scientific research" (p. 255), though in quite a different way from the one he had in mind.

It is not that psychoanalysis might be spiritual, at times, with some analysts, but that it is essentially so. The analyst does not need to pray, meditate or be in any way actively spiritual in how he or she analyses, as psychoanalysis itself is rooted in spirituality. It is not because our culture has become more appreciative of spirituality that today we can allow psychoanalysis to be more sensitive to it as well – but rather, that the spiritual was always at the *core* of psychoanalysis and the only change is that now we are starting to become more aware of it. As Gordon (2004) put it, "there has been an insistent spiritual presence in psychoanalysis, from its inception through today, which has been systemically underappreciated, but is so powerful that it continually reasserts itself" (pp. 31–32).

Beyond that, as this book demonstrated, spiritually sensitive psychoanalysis does not just focus on subjective-mystical experiences, whose relation to "truth" and "reality" is hard to evaluate. It also (and perhaps – mainly) aims at ethical, moral, social goals, at changing patterns of belief and of relating and at diminishing excessive self-involvement, which causes suffering (and its own kind of detachment from "reality").

Another criticism would concern the suggestive or directive element that might be found in spiritually sensitive psychoanalysis, which contrasts the common view of psychoanalysis as a neutral act, devoid of ideology or positive direction. Bass (1998) claimed that psychoanalysis cannot hold on to a systemized, encompassing worldview, such as the religious/spiritual one for instance. "Whenever one finds systemacity," he wrote, "one can, from a psychoanalytic point of view, ask the question of what unbearable piece of reality is being defended against by means of the system" (p. 426).

This might be true in theory, but it seems there is no real option of having no systemacity at all. Any analyst, wrote Sandler and Dreher (1996), carries personal unconscious theories, models, plans, rules for action and culturally determined values and attitudes. This is why "neutrality," they conclude, "is an ideal condition which is impossible to reach" (p. 5). Greifinger (1997) agreed, stating it is an illusion that the analyst's interventions can lay claim to a measure of "objectivity." The therapist's "way of being" in psychoanalysis, he wrote, is "shot through with suggestion" (p. 218).

This is not to say that "anything goes." The fact that absolutely no suggestion is an impossibility, does not mean we shouldn't try to get as close to that as we possibly can. It is necessary to take a measure of caution, especially in cases when only the analyst is actively involved in spirituality. In such treatments, the analyst has to be aware of his or her spiritual ambitions and aspirations, as these might arise in the countertransference. This is not different from any other expectation the analyst can have – including the wish to know better the patient's dynamics (Bollas, 1995) or even the wish that the patient get better (Bion, 1970). The same warning is also true for the traditional spiritual guru or guide. The shaman or the sheikh must respond according to the needs of the person approaching them, not their own. Spiritual traditions, unlike some institutionalized religions, are never missionary. In many traditions, like the Hindu Tantra, Islamic Sufism or Jewish Kabbalah, practitioners are even severely warned from exposing their knowledge to the uninitiated. This might be another reason why spirituality fits with the psychoanalytic outlook.

And still, one might argue, more traditional analytic goals – such as achieving "normalcy," adapting more readily to socially acceptable roles and expectations or becoming more creative or authentic – while also being based on culturally determined ideals, are more appropriate to psychoanalysis then the goals advocated by the spiritual school. Spiritually sensitive goals indeed seem to require from psychoanalysis greater elasticity than those of other schools. Specifically, the position regarding the ontological status of the self seems in sharp contrast to the basic tenets of psychoanalysis. The question is a valid one: can we broaden our scope to incorporate spiritual ideas and ideals, and remain psychoanalytic?

Rangell (2006) wrote about a "total composite analytic theory," which will be "unified and cumulative" (p. 231). Such a theory, he wrote, should encircle a variety of dichotomies: past and present, cognition and affect, intrapsychic and interpersonal, drives and objects, narrative truth and historical truth. The different analytic understandings reached over the years can collect or cohere cumulatively, Rangell suggested. Continuing this line of thought, we can expect that as a comprehensive psychoanalytic theory relates to both consciousness and the unconscious, rationality and imagination, it should, for instance, focus on the self and also take in account "self-lessness" (Rubin, 1997, p. 102).

Selflessness, to continue with this example, isn't necessarily developmentally "higher" than other, self-enhanced positions achieved by analysis. Spiritually sensitive psychoanalysis offers here just another option of looking at the self, which can be used with relevant patients. In the same way, it offers an understanding of faith and mystical experiences as possible expressions of mental health, in addition to existing formulations of them as expressions of illusion or regression.

As Aner Govrin (2016) pointed out, it is thanks to its capacities of incorporation and expansion that psychoanalysis gained its senior position in the field of investigating the psyche, over other competing theories which it managed to contain and integrate within itself (see also Wallerstein, 1988). The broadening of the limits of psychoanalytic theory, practice and goals described in this book is another important contribution of spiritual-sensitivity to psychoanalysis. Of course, this does not conceal the remaining points of friction with traditional analytic thought, or the many theoretical gaps in the new, rising approach which are to be filled.

One last conundrum. If a spiritually sensitive analysis is a process that aims at increasing compassion and love, diminishing self-interest and even sometimes getting nearer to the numinous, one might ask if there is any difference between this practice and ancient spiritual traditions. Eigen (2001b) described a treatment which was characterized by prominent spiritual elements and wondered – "Why couldn't my patient get better by going to a shaman, or a spiritual healer, or dipping into a traditional spiritual path? Why was seeing me necessary? Does psychoanalytic therapy add anything to the Light?" (p. 36). Even if it does, how does it differ from older "spiritually sensitive" therapeutic approaches, like Transpersonal Psychology or Jung's Analytic Psychology?[1]

The borders are indeed blurry. And yet, even if there are points and areas of overlap and interface, there are essential differences in technique, in setting, in language and in goals.

Meissner (2008) wrote about the different means religion and psychoanalysis use to attempt to heal an innate experiential fracture. Even in areas where these two have a common interest, religion (Christianity, in Meissner's case) deals with them using preaching, prayer, spiritual motivation, confession and other techniques of inspiration and forgiveness, while psychoanalysis uses associations, interpretations and emotional involvement and interaction through transference. In the Buddhist context, De Wit (2008) emphasized the differences in dealing with a necessary existential suffering, as does Buddhist doctrine, and with personal neurotic suffering, as psychoanalytic theory does. This is why, De Wit concluded, "spiritual teachers are not psychotherapists and vice versa" (p. 581).

Spiritually sensitive psychoanalysis is close to spiritual traditions, and also to "spiritual" therapies, but it isn't completely, or only spiritual. The sobering, realistic heritage left by Freud and his followers helps it retain a delicate and rare balance between spiritual attunement and a clear analytic view, which recognizes destructive unconscious forces quite often hiding behind masks of faith, mysticism or morality.

It is not just that psychoanalysis can best serve to avoid spiritual traps and bypasses. The profound knowledge of what could be *mistakenly* understood as "unspiritual" allows for psychoanalysis to make its greatest contributions to the spiritual. A true spiritual path includes and embraces its obstacles instead of trying to evade or escape them. Learning about the unconscious, getting familiar with it presence, may be a step toward enlightenment, wrote Fromm (1960). The psychoanalytic concern with building a cohesive and integrated self, Rubin (1997) stressed, is a precondition of the subsequent task of disidentifying from restrictive self-representations and reducing excessive self-involvement. As he wrote, "One certainly cannot disidentify from what one is not" (p. 101). The deep care for the bruised self that psychoanalysis offers is not separated from the liberation from a narcissistic attachment to it.

Psychoanalysis, as I demonstrated, could indeed be seen as a "spiritual practice," but it isn't completely or exclusively spiritual. The combination with its other aspects is unique, allowing a delicate, rare, balance between spiritual attunement and a sober seeing.

Freud (1921) warned of two kinds of mistakes – "the Scylla of under-estimating the importance of the repressed unconscious, and the Charybdis of judging the normal entirely by the standards of the pathological" (p. 138). The same could be said to apply to spirituality: One has to eschew both an *a priori* pathologization that automatically rejects any spiritual expression, as well as an idealization that accepts favourably any expression of spirituality without critical examination. If psychoanalysis has to date been more likely to commit the first mistake, spiritual approaches and non-analytic, spiritually orientated therapies all too often commit the second.

Spiritually sensitive psychoanalysis might manage to avoid both errors. As part of the long psychoanalytic tradition, it is more likely to notice and avoid spiritual traps such as encouraging attempts to transcend the self that are in fact based on an evasion of subjectivity. As spiritually sensitive, it can refrain from therapeutic traps such as an over-emphasis on the self, which could lead to an increase in the dynamic importance of narcissism. As an analytic-spiritual endeavour, it can see that a consolidated sense of self and a sense of non-self-centricity are *interpenetrating aspects* of human experience, and not hierarchically ordered stages (Rubin, 1997).

Indeed, *the balancing* of pathology and transcendence, human and divine, sacred and mundane, could be seen as *the* spiritual *par excellence*. This is perhaps most fully and convincingly expressed in Eigen's writings. He dives into the depths of suffering, degradation, annihilation, catastrophe, to discover Light at the centre. Both sides, Eigen (1998b) found, are not separate from each other: "It is quite a remarkable fact of life that suffering and ecstasy rest in one another" (p. 167). Or as Heraclitus wrote: "The way up and the way down are one and the same" (quoted in Mitchell, 1991, p. 9).

Eigen (2009) mentioned Pascal, who described the disproportionality of the human condition: "We are too big and too small for ourselves, behind and ahead of ourselves" (p. 7). In an analysis he performed, at the point of maximum contraction Eigen and his patient were "astonished by a radiant 'I-kernel'" (Eigen & Govrin, 2007, p. 66). Contraction *and* Light. Not contraction and then light. Suffering does not disappear, but in it, with it, light can be found, praise be given:

> The kind of damage we are talking about doesn't go away. One doesn't throw off one's crutches and sing praises to the Lord. One praises the Lord in the center of our gnarled selves, hunched over crutches we can't get rid of, that won't let go of us. Perhaps we might be able to live without them if we dared or knew how to, but that's a little like saying we might be able to live without oxygen if we weren't creatures who breathed.
> (Eigen, 2007, p. 92)

Awareness of pain and destruction exists also in other spiritual traditions and other therapies. The first noble truth of the Buddha is that life is characterized by suffering and discontent. For spiritually sensitive psychoanalysis, however, the awareness of suffering isn't moved aside for the aspiration to get free of it, which becomes the focus of spiritual practice (the next three Buddhist truths). Knowing personal suffering, a field in which psychoanalysis gained tremendous expertise and insight in over a hundred years of tenacious observation, investigation and attention, always remains a central point. This intimate acquaintance with suffering is now understood as spiritual in itself.

Spiritually sensitive psychoanalysis isn't spiritual at times, psychological at others. It is both. It isn't immersed in tribulations and then uplifted to ecstatic stratospheres. It is both. The journey is "psychospiritual," and as Eigen (1998b) wrote – we have no idea where it will take us. It can lead to childhood trauma as much as to "inklings of future possibilities, recounting past lives" (p. 225). It is always both secular and sacred. Spirituality and therapy are both embraced in a seamless way, each feeding currents of the other, the two currents being "part of one vision, one sense of the way life speaks to life" (Eigen, 2005, p. ix). A famous Zen saying noted: after the ecstasy, the laundry. Spiritually sensitive psychoanalysis might slightly adjust the proverb: during laundry, ecstasy, and vice versa.

Adam Phillips (1994), while discussing Nina Coltart's work, described psychoanalysis as an "inescapably moral enterprise," which has thus "[to] work hard not to become a moralistic one" (p. 139). No doubt, "spiritual" psychoanalytic writing fails in this work at times. In other cases, it can be intellectually unsound, infected with naïve optimism and tend to only strengthen Freud's claim that religion is nothing but an illusion created as a defence from the horrors of human existence. At its best, however, a capacity to integrate sensitivity to the spiritual with the sharp clarity of psychoanalytic lens, creates a new synthesis, which offers as wide and full a picture of the human condition and its potentials as has, perhaps, ever been realized.

In a brilliant essay, Totton (2011) claimed the shift psychoanalysis went through, from being part of medical science to acknowledging its inherent spirituality, was unavoidable, as it revealed its true nature. Psychoanalysis cannot be part of "mental medicine," Totton wrote, the analogy between physical illness and mental disturbances being "worse than dubious" (p. 145).[2] Totton's argument is that "psychoanalysis is most appropriately positioned as an *enlightenment practice*: alongside such other practices as they occur within Buddhism, within Hinduism, within Islam, within Taoism, within Judaism, within Christianity; and in few other settings" (p. 147).

Psychoanalysis is not similar to Buddhism, Hinduism, etc., Totton (2011) continued, but all "enlightenment practices," including psychoanalysis, hold some common shared features. First, they all involve *practice* – not just a theory or faith but also a technique, the aim of which is to create some change in human life. This change is described in different ways by the various practices, but all, it seems, will agree that it includes "a *radical lessening of anxiety:* a profound relaxation, which follows from a reappraisal of our situation as human beings" (p. 148).[3]

I can think of no better way to conclude than by citing mystic and analyst Michael Eigen's (2001a) beautiful description of this "enlightening" side of psychoanalysis:

> We try to get past our minds and bodies to the heart of life – hit the home run, score the touchdown, not just a matter of material success, not just saying I'm good, I'm good, but touching the thing itself, the thing that makes this all go. Can we, ought we to stop doing this? For some of us, psychoanalysis has become part of this sweeping through things, this pressure of discovery.
>
> (p. 473)

Notes

1. Spiritually sensitive psychoanalysis is indeed influenced by Analytic Psychology (see Samuels, 1996; Stephens, 1999).
2. Freud (1926) himself wrote that psychoanalysis "is not a specialized branch of medicine" and that he "cannot see how it is possible to dispute this" (p. 252).
3. Interestingly, the repression or neglect of the enlightening part by psychoanalysis is also common to other "enlightenment practices," which distanced themselves from this awareness into "institutionalization, religion, superstition, even bureaucracy" (Totton, 2011, p. 149).

References

Adler, E., & Bachant, J.L. (1996). Free association and analytic neutrality: The basic structure of the psychoanalytic situation. *Journal of the American Psychoanalytic Association*, 44, 1021–1046.

Akhtar, S. (Ed.) (2005). *Freud along the Ganges: Psychoanalytic reflections on the people and culture of India*. New York: Other Press

Akhtar, S. (Ed.) (2008). *The crescent and the couch: Cross-currents between Islam and psychoanalysis*. New York: Jason Aronson.

Alexander, F. (1931). Buddhistic training as an artificial catatonia (the biological meaning of psychic occurrences). *Psychoanalytic Review*, 18, 129–145.

Altman, N. (2007). Integrating the transpersonal with the intersubjective. *Contemporary Psychoanalysis*, 43, 526–535.

Arnowitz, Y. (2010). The Jew for Jesus and other analytic explorations of God. In: L. Aron & L. Henik (Eds.), *Answering a question with a question: Contemporary psychoanalysis and Jewish thought* (pp. 57–79). Brighton: Academic Studies Press.

Aron, L. (1996). *A meeting of minds: Mutuality in psychoanalysis*. Hillsdale: Analytic Press.

Aronowitz, S. (1988). *Science as power: Discourse and ideology in modern society*. Minneapolis, MN: University of Minnesota Press.

Bader, M.J. (1998). Postmodern epistemology: The problem of validation and the retreat from therapeutics in psychoanalysis. *Psychoanalytic Dialogues*, 8, 1–32.

Bakan, D. (1958). *Sigmund Freud and the Jewish mystical tradition*. London: Free Association Books (1990).

Balint, M. (1968). *The basic fault*. London: Tavistock.

Bar Nes, A. (2021). *Psychoanalysis, mysticism and the problem of epistemology: Defining the indefinable*. New York: Routledge.

Barnes, P.M., Bloom, B. & Nahin, R.L. (2008). Complementary and alternative medicine use among adults and children: United States, 2007. *National Health Statistic Report*, 12, 1–23.

Barnett, A.J. (2008). What is the theoretical yield in studying the psychoanalyst's intentions? *Psychoanalytic Review*, 95, 873–884.

Bass, A. (1998). Sigmund Freud. The questions of a Weltanschauung and of defense. In: P. Marcus & A. Rosenberg (Eds.), *Psychoanalytic versions of the human condition: Philosophies of life and their impact on practice* (pp. 412–446). New York: New York University Press.

Bass, A. (2001). It takes one to know one; Or, whose unconscious is it anyway? *Psychoanalytic Dialogues*, 11, 683–702.

Bauman, Z. (2000). *Liquid modernity*. Cambridge: Polity.

Becker, E. (1973). *The denial of death*. New York: Free press.

Bell, D. 2009. Is truth an illusion? Psychoanalysis and postmodernism. *The International Journal of Psychoanalysis*, 90, 331–345.

Benjamin, J. (1988). *The bonds of love: Psychoanalysis, feminism, and the problem of domination*. New York: Pantheon Books.

Berke, J.H., & Schneider, S. (2003). Repairing worlds: An exploration of the psychoanalytical and kabbalistic concepts of reparation and *Tikkun*. *Psychoanalytic Review*, 90, 723–749.

Bettelheim, B. (1982). *Freud and man's soul*. London: Pimlico.

Bielawka, M. (2009). Camus and Tischner: In search of absolute love. In: A. Tymieniecka (Ed.), *Phenomenology and existentialism in the twentieth century book two: Fruition-cross-pollination-dissemination* (pp. 147–160). New York: Springer.

Binswanger, L. (1957). *Sigmund Freud: Reminiscences of a friendship*. Guterman, N. (Trans.) New York: Grune & Stratton.

Bion, W.R. (1965). *Transformations: Change from learning to growth*. London: Heinemann.

Bion, W.R. (1970). *Attention and interpretation: A scientific approach to insight in psycho-analysis and groups*. New York: Jason Aronson.

Bion, W.R. (1992). *Cogitations*. Bion, F. (Ed.). London: Karnac Books.

Black, D.M. (2006). Introduction. In: D. M. Black (Ed.), *Psychoanalysis and religion in the 21st century: Competitors or collaborators?* (pp. 1–20). London: Routledge.

Bland, E.D. & Strawn, B.D. (Eds.) (2014) *Christianity & psychoanalysis: A new conversation*. Downers Grove: IntraVarsity Press.

Blass, R.B. (2004). Beyond illusion: Psychoanalysis and the question of religious truth. *International Journal of Psychoanalysis*, 85, 615–634.

Blechner, M. (1998). The analysis and creation of dream meaning: Interpersonal, intrapsychic, and neurobiological perspectives. *Contemporary Psychoanalysis*, 34, 181–194.

Blechner, M. (2013) New ways of conceptualizing and working with dreams. *Contemporary Psychoanalysis*, 49, 259–275.

Bleger, J. (1967). Psycho-analysis of the psycho-analytic frame. *International Journal of Psycho-Analysis*, 48, 511–519.

Bobrow, J. (Ed.) (2020). *Zen and psychotherapy: Partners in liberation*. Somerville: Wisdom.

Bohm, D. (1980). *Wholeness and the implicate order*. London: Routledge.

Bollas, C. (1995). *Cracking up: The work of unconscious experience*. London: Routledge.

Brottman, M. (2009). Psychoanalysis and magic: Then and now. *American Imago*, 66, 471–489.

Brown, R.S. (2020). *Groundwork for a transpersonal psychoanalysis: Spirituality, relationship, and participation*. London: Routledge.

Caplan, M. (2009). *Eyes wide open: cultivating discernment on the spiritual path*. Sounds True.

Carpelan, H. (1981). On the importance of the setting in the psychoanalytic situation. *Scandinavian Psychoanalytic Review*, 4, 151–160.

Celenza, A. (2007). Analytic love and power: Responsiveness and responsibility. *Psychoanalytic Inquiry*, 27, 287–301.

Cernovsky, Z. (1988). Psychoanalysis and Tibetan Buddhism as techniques of liberation. *American Journal of Psychoanalysis*, 48, 56–71.

Charles, M. (2017). The promise of love revisited: Healing ruptures through recognition. *Psychoanalytic Psychology*, 34, 186–194.

Chessick, R.D. (1997). Malignant eroticized countertransference. *Journal of the American Academy of Psychoanalytic Dynamic Psychiatry*, 25, 219–235.

Coen, S.J. (1994). Barriers to love between patient and analyst. *Journal of the American Psychoanalytic Association*, 42, 1107–1135.

Cohen, M. (2003). The affirmation of religious (not merely spiritual!) orientation in clinical treatment. *Journal of the American Academy of Psychoanalytic Dynamic Psychiatry*, 31, 269–273.

Cohen, Y. (2006). Loving the patient as the basis for treatment. *American Journal of Psychoanalysis*, 66, 139–155.

Coltart, N. (1991). The silent patient. *Psychoanalytic Dialogues*, 1, 439–453.

Coltart, N. (1992). *Slouching towards Bethlehem … and further psychoanalytic explorations.* London: Free Association Books.

Cooper, A.M. (1985). A historical review of psychoanalytic paradigms. In: A. Rothstein, (Ed.), *Models of the mind: Their relationships to clinical work* (pp. 5–20). Madison: International Universities Press.

Cooper, P. (2002). Between wonder and doubt: Psychoanalysis in the goal-free zone. *American Journal of Psychoanalysis*, 62, 95–118.

Cooper, S.H. (2000). Mutual containment in the analytic situation. *Psychoanalytic Dialogues*, 10, 169–194.

Cunningham, M. (2006). Vedanta and psychoanalysis. In: D.M. Black (Ed.), *Psychoanalysis and religion in the 21st century: Competitors or collaborators?* (pp. 234–251). London: Routledge.

Cushman, P. (1994). Confronting Sullivan's spider. *Contemporary Psychoanalysis*, 30, 800–845.

Cushman, P. (1995). *Constructing the self, constructing America: A cultural history of psychotherapy.* Reading, MA: Addison-Wesley Publishing Company.

Dan, J. (1993). In quest of a historical definition of mysticism. *Studies in Spirituality*, 3, 58–90.

Davies, J.M. (1994). Love in the afternoon: A relational reconsideration of desire and dread in the countertransference. *Psychoanalytic Dialogues*, 4, 153–170.

De Mello Franco, O.F. (1998). Religious experience and psychoanalysis: From man-as-God to man-with-God. *International Journal of Psychoanalysis*, 79, 113–131.

De Wit, H.F. (2008). Working with existential and neurotic suffering. In: F.J. Kaklauskas, S. Nimanheminda, L. Hoffman & J.S. MacAndrew (Eds.), *Brilliant sanity: Buddhist approaches to psychotherapy* (pp. 3–18). Colorado Springs: University of the Rockies Press.

Deacon, T.W. (2012). *Incomplete nature: How mind emerged from matter*. New York: W.W. Norton & Company.

DiCarlo, R.E. (1996). *Towards a new world view: Conversations on the leading edge*. Edinburgh: Floris Books.

Domash, L. (2009). The emergence of hope: Implicit spirituality in treatment and the occurrence of psychoanalytic luck. *Psychoanalytic Review*, 96, 35–54.

Duerlinger, J. (1984). *Ultimate reality and spiritual discipline*. New York: Paragon House.

Durkheim, E. (1912). *The elementary forms of the religious life*. Swain, J.W. (Trans.) London: George Allen & Unwin (1964).

Dworkin, R. (2013). *Religion without God*. Cambridge: Harvard University Press.

Eigen, M. (1981). The area of faith in Winnicott, Lacan and Bion. *International Journal of Psycho-Analysis*, 62, 413–433.

Eigen, M. (1992). *The electrified tightrope*. Northvale: Jason Aronson.

Eigen, M. (1998a). One reality. In: A. Molino (Ed.), *The couch and the tree: Dialogues in psychoanalysis and Buddhism* (pp. 217–230). New York: North Point Books.

Eigen, M. (1998b). *The psychoanalytic mystic*. London: Free Association Books

Eigen, M. (1998c). Wilfred R. Bion: Infinite surfaces, explosiveness, faith. In: P. Marcus & A. Rosenberg (Eds.), *Psychoanalytic versions of the human condition: Philosophies of life and their impact on practice* (pp. 183–205). New York: New York University Press.

Eigen, M. (2001a). Mysticism and psychoanalysis. *Psychoanalytic Review*, 88, 455–481.

Eigen, M. (2001b). *Ecstasy*. Middletown: Wesleyan University Press.

Eigen, M. (2004). *The sensitive self*. Middletown: Wesleyan University Press.

Eigen, M. (2005). Foreword. In: M.B. Weiner & C. Barbre (Eds.), *Psychotherapy and religion: Many paths, one journey* (pp. ix–x). Lanham: Jason Aronson.

Eigen, M. (2007). *Feeling matters*. London: Karnac.

Eigen, M. (2009). *Flames from the unconscious: Trauma, madness, and faith*. London: Karnac Books.

Eigen, M. (2012). *Kabbalah and psychoanalysis*. London: Karnac.

Eigen, M., & Govrin, A. (2007). *Conversations with Michael Eigen*. London: Karnac Books.

Eissler, K.R. (1965). *Medical orthodoxy and the future of psychoanalysis*. New York: International Universities Press.

El Shakry, O. (2017). *The Arabic Freud: Psychoanalysis and Islam in modern Egypt*. Princeton: Princeton University Press.

Elliott, A., & Spezzano, C. (1996). Psychoanalysis at its limits: Navigating the postmodern turn. *Psychoanalytic Quarterly*, 65, 52–83.

Epstein, M. (1995). *Thoughts without a thinker: Psychotherapy from a Buddhist perspective*. New York: Basic Books.

Epstein, M. (2001). *Going on being: Buddhism and the way of change, a positive psychology for the West*. New York: Continuum.

Erikson, E.H. (1958). *Young man Luther: A study in psychoanalysis and history*. London: Faber and Faber.

Erikson, E.H. (1969). *Gandhi's truth: On the origins of militant non violence*. London: Faber and Faber.

Eshel, O. (2019). *The emergence of analytic oneness: Into the heart of psychoanalysis*. New York: Routledge.

Esman, A.H. (2003). Psychoanalysis and "spirituality". *Journal of Clinical Psychoanalysis*, 12, 85–103.

Etezady, M.H. (2008). Faith and the couch: A psychoanalytic perspective on transformation. *Psychoanalytic Inquiry*, 28, 560–569.

Fadiman, C. (Ed.) (1990). *Living philosophies: The reflections of some eminent men and women of our time*. New York: Doubleday.

Fairbairn, W.R.D. (1952). *Psychoanalytic studies of the personality*. London: Routledge & Kegan Paul.

Falzeder, E. (1994). My grand patient, my chief tormentor: A hitherto unnoticed case of Freud's and the consequences. *Psychoanalytic Quarterly*, 63, 297–331.

Fauteux, K. (1997). Self-reparation in religious experience and creativity. In: C. Spezzano & G.J. Gargiulo (Eds.), *Soul on the couch: Spirituality, religion, and morality in contemporary psychoanalysis* (pp. 11–41). Hillsdale: Analytic Press.

Feiler, B. (2014). The new allure of sacred pilgrimages. *New York Times*, 20 December.

Fenichel, O. (1939). Problems of psychoanalytic technique. *Psychoanalytic Quarterly*, 7, 303–324.

Ferenczi, S. (1932/1988). *The clinical diary of Sandor Ferenczi*. Cambridge, MA: Harvard University Press.

Ferenczi, S. (1934/1949). Confusion of the tongues between the adults and the child (the language of tenderness and of passion). *International Journal of Psycho-Analysis*, 30, 225–230.

Field, N. (1999). 'O tell me the truth about love'. In D. Mann (Ed.), *Erotic transference and countertransference: Clinical practice in psychotherapy* (pp. 91–101). New York: Routledge.

Fink, B. (2015). Love and/in psychoanalysis: A commentary on Lacan's reading of Plato's symposium in seminar VIII: Transference. *Psychoanalytic Review*, 102, 59–91.

Finn, M. (2003). Tibetan Buddhism and a mystical psychoanalysis. In: J.D. Safran (Ed.), *Psychoanalysis and Buddhism: An unfolding dialogue* (pp. 101–115). Somerville: Wisdom Publications.

Flynn Campbell, E. (2005). Psychotherapy and the sacred. In: B. Marcella & C. Barbre (Eds.), *Psychotherapy and religion: Many paths, one journey* (pp. 57–76). Lanham: Jason Aronson.

Forman, R.K.C. (1999). *Mysticism, mind, consciousness*. Albany: State University of New York Press.

Forman, R.K.C. (2004). *Grassroots spirituality: What it is, why it is here, where it is going*. Exeter & Charlottesville: Imprint Academic.

Fosshage, J.L. (2007). Searching for love and expecting rejection: Implicit and explicit dimensions in cocreating analytic change. *Psychoanalytic Inquiry*, 27, 326–347.

Frank, G. (1987). Weinstein revisited: Should analysts love their patients? *Modern Psychoanalysis*, 12, 89–95.

Freud, S. (1900). *The interpretation of dreams. SE* 4 & 5. London: Hogarth.

Freud, S. (1901). *The psychopathology of everyday life. SE* 5.

Freud, S. (1907). Obsessive actions and religious practices. *SE*, 9, 115–128.

Freud, S. (1909). Letter from Sigmund Freud to C.G. Jung, April 16, 1909. *The Freud/Jung letters: The correspondence between Sigmund Freud and C.G. Jung*, 218–220.

Freud, S. (1910). Leonardo Da Vinci and a memory of his childhood. *SE*, 11, 57–138.

Freud, S. (1912). Recommendations to physicians practising psycho-analysis. *SE*, 12, 109–120.

Freud, S. (1913). On beginning the treatment. *SE*, 12, pp. 123–144.

Freud, S. (1915). Observations on transference-love (further recommendations on the technique of psycho-analysis III). *SE*, 12, 157–171.

Freud, S. (1917). Introductory lectures on psycho-analysis, part III: General theory of the neuroses. *SE*, 16, 243–477.

Freud, S. (1918). From the history of an infantile neurosis. *SE*, 17, 1–124.

Freud, S. (1921 [1941]). Psycho-analysis and telepathy. *SE*, 18, 175–193.

Freud, S. (1922). Dreams and telepathy. *SE*, 22, 195–220.

Freud, S. (1923). Two encyclopedia articles. *SE*, 18, 233–260.

Freud, S. (1926). The question of lay analysis. *SE*, 20, 177–258.

Freud, S. (1927). The future of an illusion. *SE*, 21, 5–56.

Freud, S. (1930). Civilization and its discontents. *SE*, 21, 64–148.

Freud, S. (1933a). The dissection of the psychical personality. *SE*, 22, 57–80.

Freud, S. (1933b). The question of a weltanschauung. *SE*, 22, 158–182.

Freud, S. (1935). Postscript. In: *An autobiographical study. SE*, 20, 71–74.

Freud, S. (1937). Letter to Marie Bonaparte, August 13, 1937. In: E.L. Freud (Ed.), *Letters of Sigmund Freud 1873–1939* (pp. 436–437). London: Hogarth Press (1961).

Freud, S., & Breuer, J. (1895). *Studies on hysteria*. In J. Strachey (Ed. & Trans.), *The standard edition of the psychological works of Sigmund Freud (SE)*, Vol. 2. London: Hogarth Press.

Freud, S., & Pfister, O. (1963). *Psychoanalysis and faith: The letters of Sigmund Freud and Oskar Pfister*. E.L. Freud & H. Meng (Eds.), E. Mosbacher (Trans.) New York: Basic Books.

Frie, R. (2012). Psychoanalysis, religion, philosophy and the possibility for dialogue: Freud, Binswanger and Pfister. *International Forum of Psychoanalysis*, 21, 106–116.

Friedman, L. (2005). Is there a special psychoanalytic love? *Journal of the American Psychoanalytic Association*, 53, 349–375.

Fromm, E. (1950). *Psychoanalysis and religion*. New Haven: Yale University Press.

Fromm, E. (1956). The present human condition. In: *The dogma of Christ and other essays on religion, psychology and culture* (pp. 95–105). New York: Holt, Rinehart and Winston (1963).

Fromm, E. (1960). Psychoanalysis and Zen Buddhism. In: D.T. Suzuki, E. Fromm & R. de Martino (Eds.), *Zen Buddhism and psychoanalysis* (pp. 77–141). New York: Harper.

Fromm, E. (1966). *You shall be as Gods: A radical interpretation of the Old Testament and its tradition*. New York: Holt, Rinehart and Winston.

Fukuyama, F. (1999). *The great disruption: Human nature and the reconstitution of social order*. New York: The Free Press.

Gargiulo, G.J. (1997). Inner mind/outer mind and the quest for the "I": Spirituality revisited. In: C. Spezzanos & G.J. Gargiulo. (Eds.), *Soul on the couch: Spirituality, religion, and morality in contemporary psychoanalysis* (pp. 1–9). Hillsdale: Analytic Press.

Gay, P. (1987). *A godless Jew: Freud, atheism, and the making of psychoanalysis*. New Haven: Yale University Press.

Gellner, E. (1985). *The psychoanalytic movement or the cunning of unreason*. Oxford: Blackwell (2003).

Genoud, C. (2006). *Gesture of awareness: A radical approach to time, space, and movement*. Somerville: Wisdom Publications.

Gerrard, J. (2005). Love in the time of psychotherapy. In D. Mann (Ed.), *Erotic transference and countertransference: Clinical practice in psychotherapy* (pp. 21–41). New York: Routledge.

Ghent, E. (1990). Masochism, submission, surrender—Masochism as a perversion of surrender. *Contemporary Psychoanalysis*, 26, 108–136.

Giddens, A. (1992). *The transformation of intimacy: Sexuality, love and eroticism in modern societies*. Stanford: Stanford University Press.

Gordon, K. (2004). The tiger's stripe: Some thoughts on psychoanalysis, gnosis, and the experience of wonderment. *Contemporary Psychoanalysis*, 40, 5–45.

Gordon, K. (2006). Reading Michael Eigen. *Contemporary Psychoanalysis*, 42, 107–118.

Gottesfeld, M.L. (1985). Mystical aspects of psychotherapeutic efficacy. *Psychoanalytic Review*, 72, 589–597.

Govrin, A. (2006). The dilemma of contemporary psychoanalysis: Toward a "knowing" post-postmodernism. *Journal of the American Psychoanalytic Association*, 54, 507–535.

Govrin, A. (2016). *Conservative and radical perspectives in psychoanalysis: The fascinated and the disenchanted*. London: Routledge.

Green, A. (1975). The analyst, symbolization and absence in the analytic setting (on changes in analytic practice and analytic experience)—In memory of D. W. Winnicott. *International Journal of Psycho-Analysis*, 56, 1–22.

Greifinger, J. (1997). On the horizon of authenticity: Toward a moral account of psychoanalytic therapy. In: C. Spezzano & G.J. Gargiulo (Eds.), *Soul on the couch: Spirituality, religion, and morality in contemporary psychoanalysis* (pp. 201–230). Hillsdale: Analytic Press.

Grotstein, J.S. (2000). *Who is the dreamer who dreams the dream? A study of psychic presences*. London: Routledge.

Grotstein, J.S. (2006). Forward: The case for the numinous. In: A. Casement & D. Tacey (Eds.), *The idea of the numinous: Contemporary Jungian and psychoanalytic perspectives* (pp. xi–xv). London & New York: Routledge.

Hadar, U. (2013). *Psychoanalysis and social involvement: Interpretation and action*. New York: Palgrave Macmillan.

Hale, N.G. Jr. (1995). *The rise and crisis of psychoanalysis in the United States: Freud and the Americans, 1917-1985*. New York: Oxford University Press.

Hartmann, H. (1939a). *Ego psychology and the problem of adaptation*. D. Rapaport (Trans.). London: Imago Publishing (1958).

Hassan, I. (2001). From postmodernism to postmodernity: The local/global context. *Philosophy and Literature*, 25, 1–13.

Heelas, P. (1996). *The new age movement: The celebration of the self and the sacralization of modernity*. Oxford: Blackwell.

Heelas, P. (2008). *Spiritualities of life: New age romanticism and consumptive capitalism*. Malden: Blackwell.

Hernández-Tubert, R. (2008). Contribution to the discussion on the analytic frame. *Psychoanalytic Dialogues*, 18, 248–251.

Herrick, J.A. (2003). *The making of the new spirituality: The eclipse of the Western religious tradition*. Downers Grove: InterVarsity Press.

Hoffer, A. (1993). Is love in the analytic relationship "real"? *Psychoanalytic Inquiry*, 13, 343–356.

Hoffman, I.Z. (1993). The intimate authority of the psychoanalyst's presence. *Psychologist Psychoanalyst*, 13, 15–23.

Hoffman, I.Z. (2009). Therapeutic passion in the countertransference. *Psychoanalytic Dialogues*, 19, 617–637.

Hoffman, M.T. (2004). From enemy combatant to strange bedfellow: The role of religious narratives in the work of W.R.D. Fairbairn and D.W. Winnicott. *Psychoanalytic Dialogues*, 14, 769–804.

Hoffman, M.T. (2010). *Toward mutual recognition: Relational psychoanalysis and the Christian narrative*. New York: Routledge.

Hoffman, M. T. (2020) Christianity and psychoanalysis: Orienting view and augmenting modality. *Psychoanalytic Inquiry*, 40, 395–407.

Hollenback, J.B. (1996). *Mysticism: Experience, response, and empowerment*. Pennsylvania: Pennsylvania State University Press.

Hood, B. (2012). *Self illusion: Why there is no 'you' inside your head*. London: Constable.

Huguelet, P. & Koenig, H.G. (Eds.) (2009). *Religion and spirituality in psychiatry*. Cambridge: Cambridge University Press.

Hutcheon, L. (2002). *The politics of postmodernism* (2nd edition). London: Routledge.

Huxley, A. (1946). *The perennial philosophy*. London: Chatto & Windus.

James, W. (1902). *The varieties of religious experience: A study in human nature*. London: Longmans.

Jones, E. (1957). *Sigmund Freud life and work, volume three: The last phase 1919-1939*. London: Hogarth Press.

Jones, J.W. (2007). The return of the repressed: Narcissism, religion, and the ferment in psychoanalysis. *Annual of Psychoanalysis*, 35, 47–60.

Jung, C.G. (1933). *Modern man in search of a soul*. Dell, W.S. & Baynes, C.F. (Trans.) London: Routledge & Kegan Paul (1966).

Jung, C.G. (1934). The state of psychotherapy today. *Collected Works (CW)*, 10, 157–173.

Jung, C.G. (1948). A psychological approach to the dogma of the trinity. *CW*, 11, 107–200.

Jung, C.G. (1952), *Synchronicity: An acausal connecting principle*. R.F.C. Hull (Trans.). Princeton: Princeton University Press.

Jurist, E.L. (2000). *Beyond Hegel and Nietzsche: Philosophy, culture, and agency*. Cambridge, MA: MIT Press.

Kant, I. (1781). *Critique of pure reason*. N. Kemp Smith (Trans.). London: Macmillan (1964).

Karasu, T.B. (1999). Spiritual psychotherapy. *American Journal of Psychotherapy*, 53, 143–161.

Kernberg, O.F. (1994). Love in the analytic setting. *Journal of the American Psychoanalytic Association*, 42, 1137–1157.

Khan, M. (1972). *The privacy of the self*. London: Hogarth Press.

Klein, J. (2004). Narcissism, the mystics' remedy. In: B. Bishop, A. Foster, J. Klein & V. O'Connell (Eds.), *Elusive elements in practice (practice of psychotherapy)* (pp. 67–88). London: Karnac.

Kohut, H. (1966). Forms and transformations of narcissism. *Journal of the American Psychoanalytic Association*, 14, 243–272.

Kubie, L.S. (1959). Psychoanalysis and scientific method. In: H. Sidney (Ed.), *Psychoanalysis, scientific method and philosophy* (pp. 57–77). New York: New York University Press.

Kulka, R. (2020). From civilization of pessimism to culture of compassion: Self psychological reflections on Freud's essay "Civilization and its discontents." *Psychoanalytic Inquiry*, 40, 288–299.

Kurtz, S. (1989). *The art of unknowing: Dimensions of openness in analytic therapy*. Northvale: Jason Aronson.

LaMothe, R. (2002). Loss and re-creation of faith in Freud's life. *Free Associations*, 9, 371–392.

LaMothe, R. (2009). The clash of gods: Changes in a patient's use of God representations. *Journal of American Academy of Psychoanalysis*, 37, 73–84.

LaMothe, R., Arnold, J. & Crane, J. (1998). The penumbra of religious discourse. *Psychoanalytic Psychology*, 15, 63–73.

Langan, R. (2003). The dissolving of dissolving itself. In: J.D. Safran (Ed.), *Psychoanalysis and Buddhism: An unfolding dialogue* (pp. 131–146). Somerville: Wisdom Publications.

Lasch, C. (1979). *The culture of narcissism: American life in an age of diminishing expectations*. New York: Warner Books.

Lawner, P. (2001). Spiritual implications of psychodynamic therapy: Immaterial psyche, ideality, and the "area of faith". *Psychoanalytic Review*, 88, 525–548.

Lev, G. (2015). Morality, selflessness, transcendence: On treatment goals of a spiritually sensitive psychoanalysis. *Contemporary Psychoanalysis*, 51, 523–556.

Lev, G. (2016). The question of analytic aims: Psychoanalysis and the changing formulations of the life worth living. *Psychoanalytic Psychology*, 33, 312–333.

Lev, G. (2017). Getting to the heart of life: Psychoanalysis as a spiritual practice. *Contemporary Psychoanalysis*, 53, 222–246.

Lev, G. (2018). Poetics of reconcilement: Psychoanalysis and dilemmas of faith. *Psychoanalytic Psychology*, 35, 38–45.

Lev, G. (in press). The dream-like event.

Littlewood, J.E. (1986). *Littlewood's miscellany*. Cambridge: Cambridge University Press.

Loewald, H. (1970). Psychoanalytic theory and psychoanalytic process. In: *Papers on psychoanalysis* (pp. 277–301). New Haven: Yale University Press.

Loewald, H. (1978). *Psychoanalysis and the history of the individual*. New Haven: Yale University Press.

Lyotard, J. (1979). *The post-modern condition: A report on knowledge*. G. Bennington & B. Massumi (Trans.). Manchester: Manchester University Press (1984).

Magid, B. (2000). The couch and the cushion: Integrating Zen and psychoanalysis. *Journal of the American Academy of Psychoanalysis and Dynamic Psychiatry*, 28, 513–526.

Marcus, P. (2003). *Ancient religious wisdom, spirituality, and psychoanalysis*. Westport: Praeger.

Marcus, P. (2021). *Psychoanalysis as a spiritual discipline: In dialogue with Martin Buber and Gabriel Marcel*. London: Routledge.

Masters, R.A. (2010). *Spiritual bypassing: When spirituality disconnects us from what really matters*. Berkeley: North Atlantic Books.

May, S. (2011). *Love: A history*. New Haven: Yale University Press.

Mayer, E.L. (2007). *Extraordinary knowing: Science, skepticism, and the inexplicable powers of the human mind*. New York: Bantam.

Meissner, W.W. & Schlauch, C.R. (Eds.) (2003). *Psyche and spirit: Dialectics of transformation*. Lanham: University Press of America.

Meissner, W.W. (1984). *Psychoanalysis and religious experience*. New Haven: Yale University Press.

Meissner, W.W. (2008). Psychoanalysis and Catholicism – Dialogues in transformation. *Psychoanalytic Inquiry*, 28, 580–589.

Meltzer, D. (1975). Adhesive identification. *Contemporary Psychoanalysis*, 11, 289–310.

Mendelsohn, E. (2007). Analytic love: Possibilities and limitations. *Psychoanalytic Inquiry*, 27, 219–245.

Menninger, K. (1958). *Theory of psychoanalytic technique*. New York: Basic Books.

Merkur, D. (1999). *Mystical moments and unitive thinking*. Albany: State University of New York Press.

Mills, J. (2005). A critique of relational psychoanalysis. *Psychoanalytic Psychology*, 22, 155–188.

Milner, M. (1973). Some notes on psychoanalytic ideas about mysticism. In: *The suppressed madness of sane men: Forty-four years of exploring psychoanalysis* (pp. 258–274). London: Routledge (1987).

Mitchell, S. (Ed.) (1991). *The enlightened mind: An anthology of sacred prose.* New York: Harper Collins.

Mitchell S.A., & Aron, L. (1999). Editor's introduction to 'The area of faith in Winnicott, Lacan and Bion'. In: S.A. Mitchell & L. Aron (Eds.), *Relational psychoanalysis: The emergence of a tradition* (pp. 1–2). Hillsdale: Analytic Press.

Mitchell, M. (1981). The area of faith in Winnicott, Lacan and Bion. *International Journal of Psycho-Analysis*, 62, 413–433.

Mitchell, S.A. (1990). Discussion: A relational view. *Psychoanalytic Inquiry*, 10, 523–540.

Mitchell, S.A. (1993). *Hope and dread in psychoanalysis.* New York: Basic Books.

Mitrani, J.L. (2001). 'Taking the transference': Some technical implications in three papers by Bion. *International Journal of Psycho-Analysis*, 82, 1085–1104.

Modell, A.H. (1988). The centrality of the psychoanalytic setting and the changing aims of treatment—A perspective from a theory of object relations. *Psychoanalytic Quarterly*, 57, 577–596.

Molino, A., Carnevali, R. & Giannandrea, A. (Eds.) (2014). *Crossroads in psychoanalysis, Buddhism, and mindfulness: The word and the breath.* Lanham: Jason Aronson.

Moncayo, R. (1998). True subject is no-subject. *Psychoanalysis and Contemporary Thought*, 21, 383–422.

Nacht, S. (1962). The curative factors in psycho-analysis—Contributions to discussion. *International Journal of Psycho-Analysis*, 43, 233.

Natterson, J.M. (2003). Love in psychotherapy. *Psychoanalytic Psychology*, 20, 509–521.

Nerurkar, A., Yeh, G., Davis, R.B., Birdee, G., & Phillips, R.S. (2011). When conventional medical providers recommend unconventional medicine: Results of a national study. *Archives of Internal Medicine*, 171, 862–864.

Novick, J., & Novick, K.K. (2000). Love in the therapeutic alliance. *Journal of the American Psychoanalytic Association*, 48, 189–218.

Nussbaum, M.C. (2005). Analytic love and human vulnerability: A comment on Lawrence Friedman's "Is there a special psychoanalytic love?". *Journal of the American Psychoanalytic Association*, 53, 377–383.

Ogden, T.H. (2004). The analytic third: Implications for psychoanalytic theory and technique. *Psychoanalytic Quarterly*, 73, 167–195.

Oliver, T. (2020). *The self delusion: The surprising science of our connection to each other and the natural world*. London: Weidenfeld & Nicolson.

Otto, R. (1917). *The idea of the holy: An inquiry into the non-rational factor in the idea of the divine and its relation to the rational*. J. W. Harvey (Trans.). London: Oxford University Press (1950).

Palmer, M. (1997). *Freud and Jung on religion*. London: Routledge.

Pandolfo, S. (2018). *Knot of the soul: Madness, psychoanalysis, Islam*. Chicago: University of Chicago Press.

Pargament, K. I. (2007). *Spiritually integrated psychotherapy: Understanding and addressing the sacred*. New York: Guilford.

Parker, I. (1997). *Psychoanalytic culture: Psychoanalytic discourse in Western society*. London: Sage.

Parsons, W.B. (2007). Psychoanalytic spirituality. *The Annual of Psychoanalysis*, 35, 83–97.

Parsons, W.B. (2013). *Freud and Augustine in dialogue: Psychoanalysis, mysticism and the culture of modern spirituality*. Charlottesville: University of Virginia Press.

Pew Forum on Religion & Public Life (2012). *"Nones" on the rise: One-in-five adults have no religious affiliation*. www.pewforum.org.

Phillips, A. (1994). *On flirtation*. London: Faber.

Phillips, A. (1998). Reflections on Buddhism and psychoanalysis. In: A. Molino (Ed.), *The couch and the tree: Dialogues in psychoanalysis and Buddhism* (pp. 195–199). New York: North Point Books.

Plato (385–370 BCE) (2008). *Symposium*. M. C. Howatson (Trans.). Cambridge: Cambridge University Press.

Poe, E.A. (1849). Annabel lee. In: J.H. Whitty (Ed.), *The complete poems of Edgar Allan Poe* (pp. 80–81). Boston & New York: Houghton Mifflin (1911).

Ram Das (1971). *Be here now*. San Cristobal: Lama Foundation.

Rangell, L. (2006). An analysis of the course of psychoanalysis: The case for a unitary theory. *Psychoanalytic Psychology*, 23, 217–238.

Red Pine (2008). *The platform sutra: The Zen teaching of Huineng.* Berkeley: Counterpoint Press.

Renik, O. (2001). The patient's experience of therapeutic benefit. *Psychoanalytic Quarterly,* 70, 233–234.

Rieff, P. (1966). *The triumph of the therapeutic: Uses of faith after Freud.* New York: Harper & Row.

Rizzuto, A. (1979). *The birth of the living God: A psychoanalytic study.* Chicago: University of Chicago Press.

Rizzuto, A. (1998). *Why did Freud reject God? A psychoanalytic interpretation.* New Haven & London: Yale University Press.

Rizzuto, A. (2003). Believing, personal beliefs, and transformational processes: Psychoanalytic consideration. In: W.W. Meissner & C.R. Schlauch (Eds.), *Psyche and spirit: Dialectics of transformation* (pp. 1–25). Lanham: University Press of America.

Rizzuto, A. (2009). Sacred space, analytic space, the self, and God. *Journal of the American Academy of Psychoanalysis and Dynamic Psychiatry,* 37, 193–208.

Roland, A. (2003). Psychoanalysis and the spiritual quest: Framing a new paradigm. In: A. Roland, B. Ulanov & C. Barbre (Eds.), *Creative dissent: Psychoanalysis in evolution* (pp. 219–229). Westport: Praeger.

Rosenbaum, R. (2011). Exploring the other dark continent: Parallels between psi phenomena and the psychotherapeutic process. *Psychoanalytic Review,* 98, 57–90.

Rovelli, C. (1996). Relational quantum mechanics. *International Journal of Theoretical Physics,* 35, 1637–1678.

Rovelli, C. (2021). *Helgoland: Making sense of the quantum revolution.* Segre, E. & Carnell, S. (Trans.). New York: Riverhead Books.

Rubin, J.B. (1997). Psychoanalysis is self-centered. In: C. Spezzano & G.J. Gargiulo (Eds.), *Soul on the couch: Spirituality, religion, and morality in contemporary psychoanalysis* (pp. 79–108). Hillsdale: Analytic Press.

Rubin, J.B. (2004). *The good life: Psychoanalytic reflections on love, ethics, creativity and spirituality.* Albany: State University of New York Press.

Rubin, J.B. (2006). Psychoanalysis and spirituality. In: D. M. Black (Ed.), *Psychoanalysis and religion in the 21st century: Competitors or collaborators?* (pp. 132–153). London: Routledge.

Russell, B. (1917). *Mysticism and logic*. London and New York: Routledge (1994).

Rustin, M. (1999). Psychoanalysis: The last modernism. In D. Bell (Ed.), *Psychoanalysis and culture: A Kleinian perspective* (pp. 105–121). London: Gerald Duckworth & Co.

Safran, J.D. (Ed.) (2003). *Psychoanalysis and Buddhism: An unfolding dialogue*. Somerville: Wisdom Publications.

Samuels, A. (1996). Jung's return from banishment. *Psychoanalytic Review*, 83, 469–489.

Samuels, A. (2001). *Politics on the couch: Citizenship and the internal life*. New York: Other Press.

Samuels, A. (2004a). Politics on the couch?: Psychotherapy and society – some possibilities and some limitations. *Psychoanalytic Dialogues*, 14, 817–834.

Samuels, A. (2004b). A new anatomy of spirituality: Clinical and political demands the psychotherapist cannot ignore. *Psychotherapy and Politics International*, 2, 201–211.

Sandler, J., & Dreher, A.U. (1996). *What do psychoanalysts want?: The problem of aims in psychoanalytic therapy*. London: Routledge.

Sandler, E.H. & Giovannetti, M.D. (2005). Freud and Jung today. *International Journal of Psychoanalysis*, 86, 535–537.

Sass, L.A. (1992). The epic of disbelief: The postmodernist turn in contemporary psychoanalysis. In S. Kvale (Ed.), *Psychology and postmodernism* (pp. 166–182). Newbury Park: Sage Publications.

Sayers, J. (2003). *Divine therapy: Love, mysticism, and psychoanalysis*. Oxford: Oxford University Press.

Schafer, R. (1983). *The analytic attitude*. New York: Basic Books.

Schaler Buchholz, E. (2003). Freedom to choose between goodness and badness: Self-regulation and the temptation to be evil. In: A. Roland, B. Ulanov & C. Barbre (Eds.), *Creative dissent: Psychoanalysis in evolution* (pp. 231–244). Westport: Praeger.

Searles, H.F. (1959). Oedipal love in the countertransference. *International Journal of Psycho-Analysis*, 40, 180–190.

Segal, H. (1962). The curative factors in psycho-analysis— Contributions to discussion. *International Journal of Psycho-Analysis*, 43, 232–233.

Sen-Gupta, O. (2012). *The heart of practice: Understanding yoga from inside*. Jerusalem: Vijñāna Books.

Sennett, R. (1998). *The corrosion of character: The personal consequences of work in the new capitalism*. New York: W.W. Norton & Company.

Shafranske, E.P. (2005). A psychoanalytic approach to spiritually oriented psychotherapy. In L. Sperry & E.P. Shafranske (Eds.), *Spiritually oriented psychotherapy* (pp. 105–130). Washington, DC: American Psychological Association.

Shaw, D. (2003). On the therapeutic action of analytic love. *Contemporary Psychoanalysis*, 39, 251–278.

Silverberg, F. (2011). The Tao of self psychology: Was Heinz Kohut a Taoist sage?. *Psychoanalytic Inquiry*, 3, 475–488.

Simmonds, J.G. (2004). Heart and spirit: Research with psychoanalysts and psychoanalytic psychotherapists about spirituality. *International Journal of Psychoanalysis*, 85, 951–971.

Simmonds, J.G. (2006). The oceanic feeling and a sea change: Historical challenges to reductionist attitudes to religion and spirit from within psychoanalysis. *Psychoanalytic Psychology*, 23, 128–142.

Simmons, S. (2012). *I'm your man: The life of Leonard Cohen*. London: Jonathan Cape.

Smith, J.H. (1986). Primitive guilt. In J.H. Smith & W. Kerrigan (Eds.), *Pragmatism's Freud: The moral disposition of psychoanalysis* (pp. 52–78). Baltimore: The Johns Hopkins University Press.

Sorenson, R.L. (2004a). *Minding spirituality*. Hillsdale: Analytic Press.

Sorenson, R.L. (2004b). Kenosis and alterity in Christian spirituality, *Psychoanalytic Psychology*, 21, 458–462.

Spero, M.H. (1992). *Religious objects as psychological structures: A critical integration of object relations theory, psychotherapy and Judaism*. Chicago: University of Chicago Press.

Spero, M.H. (2008). The experience of religious transformation during psychoanalysis as an event horizon. *Psychoanalytic Inquiry*, 28, 622–637.

Sri Nisargadatta Maharaj (1973). *I am that*. Frydman, M. (Trans.). Mumbai: Chetana (2009).

Starr, K.E. (2008). *Repair of the soul: Metaphors of transformation in Jewish mysticism and psychoanalysis*. New York: Routledge.

Steiner, G. (1976). A note on language and psychoanalysis. *International Review of Psychoanalysis*, 3, 253–258.

Steingart, I. (1995). *A thing apart: Love and reality in the therapeutic relationship*. Northvale: Jason Aronson.

Stephens, B.D. (1999). The return of the prodigal. *Journal of Analytic Psychology*, 44, 197–220.

Stern, S. (2011). The therapeutic action of analytic love: Commentary on Joye Weisel-Barth's "Katherine: A long, hard case". *International Journal of Psychoanalytic Self Psychology*, 6, 489–504.

Stone, C. (2005). Opening psychoanalytic space to the spiritual. *Psychoanalytic Review*, 92, 417–430.

Suzuki, D.T. (1934). *Manual of Zen Buddhism*. New York: Grove Press (1960).

Suzuki, S. (1970). *Zen mind, beginner's mind*. T. Dixon (Ed.). New York & Tokyo: Weatherhill.

Swedenborg, E. (1771). *The true Christian religion: Containing the universal theology of the new church*. J. Clowes (Trans.). London: James S. Hodson (1837).

Symington, N. (1994). *Emotion and spirit: Questioning the claims of psychoanalysis and religion*. London: Cassell.

Symington, N. (2004). *The blind man sees: Freud's awakening and other essays*. London: Karnac Books.

Symington, N. (2012). The essence of psycho-analysis as opposed to what is secondary. *Psychoanalytic Dialogues*, 22, 395–409.

Szasz, T. S. (1957). On the theory of psycho-analytic treatment. *International Journal of Psychoanalysis*, 38, 166–180.

Tacey, D. (2004). *The spirituality revolution: The emergence of contemporary spirituality*. New York: HarperCollins.

Tarnus, R. (1996). The Western world view: Past, present and future. In R.E. DiCarlo (Ed.), *Towards a new world view: Conversations on the leading edge* (pp. 33–47). Edinburgh: Floris Books.

Taylor, C. (2007). *A secular age*. Cambridge: Belknap Press of Harvard University Press.

Tennes, M. (2007a). Beyond intersubjectivity: The transpersonal dimensions of the psychoanalytic encounter. *Contemporary Psychoanalysis*, 43, 505–525.

Tennes, M. (2007b). Reply to commentaries by Neil Altman and Thomas Menaker. *Contemporary Psychoanalysis*, 43, 542–553.

Thorne, B. (2011). The accountable therapist: Standards, experts and poisoning the well. In: R. House & N. Totton (Eds.), *Implausible professions: Arguments for pluralism and autonomy in psychotherapy and counselling, extended 2nd edition* (pp. 161–169). Ross-on-Wye: PCCS Books.

Tolle, E. (1997). *The power of now: A guide to spiritual enlightenment*. Novato: New World Library.

Totton, N. (2011). Not just a job: Psychotherapy as a spiritual and political practice. In: R. House & N. Totton (Eds.), *Implausible professions: Arguments for pluralism and autonomy in psychotherapy and counselling, extended 2nd edition* (pp. 145–157). Ross-on-Wye: PCCS Books.

Tubert-Oklander, J. (2008). Contribution to the discussion on the analytic frame. *Psychoanalytic Dialogues*, 18, 239–242.

Ulanov, A.B. (2000). *Finding space: Winnicott, God, and psychic reality*. Louisville: Westminster John Knox Press.

Vida, J.E. (2002). The role of love in the therapeutic action of psychoanalysis. *American Imago*, 59, 435–445.

Waaijman, K. (1993). Toward a phenomenological definition of spirituality. *Studies in Spirituality*, 3, 5–57.

Wallerstein, R.S. (1965). The goals of psychoanalysis: A survey of analytic viewpoints. *Journal of the American Psychoanalytic Association*, 13, 748–770.

Wallerstein, R.S. (1988). One psychoanalysis or many? *International Journal of Psycho-Analysis*, 69, 5–21.

Wallerstein, R.S. (1992). The goals of psychoanalysis reconsidered. In A. Sugarman, R.A. Nemiroff & D.P. Greenson (Eds.), *The technique and practice of psychoanalysis, volume II: A memorial volume to Ralph R. Greenson* (pp. 63–90). Madison, CT: International Universities Press.

Wallerstein, R.S. (2002). The growth and transformation of American ego psychology. *Journal of the American Psychoanalytic Association*, 50, 135–168.

Weinstein, R.S. (1986). Should analysts love their patients? *Modern Psychoanalysis*, 11, 103–110.

Weinstein, R.S. (2007). What heals in psychoanalysis? *Psychoanalytic Inquiry*, 27, 302–309.

West, W. (2000). *Psychotherapy and spirituality: Crossing the line between therapy and religion*. London: Sage Publications.

Winnicott, D.W. (1956). Primary maternal preoccupation. In: *Collected papers: Through paediatrics to psycho-analysis* (pp. 300–305). London: Tavistock.

Winnicott, D.W. (1965). *The maturational processes and the facilitating environment*. London: Hogarth Press & the Institute of Psycho-Analysis.

Winnicott, D.W. (1971). *Playing and reality*. London: Tavistock.

Wittgenstein, L. (1921). *Tractatus logico-philosophicus*. C.K. Ogden (Trans.). London: Routledge & Kegan Paul (1974).

Wittgenstein, L. (1953). *Philosophical investigations*. Oxford: Blackwell.

Wolson, P. (2011). The seminal therapeutic influence of analytic love: A pluralistic perspective. In: M.J. Diamond, C. Christian (Eds.), *The second century of psychoanalysis: Evolving perspectives on therapeutic action* (pp. 163–185). London: Karnac.

Woodhouse, M.B. (1996). *Paradigm wars: World-view for a new age*. Berkeley: Frog.

Wuthnow, R. (2007). *After the baby boomers: How twenty- and thirty-somethings are shaping the future of American religion*. Princeton: Princeton University Press.

Yalom, I.D. (1980). *Existential psychotherapy*. New York: Basic Books.

Young-Eisendrath, P. (2008). The transformation of human suffering: A perspective from psychotherapy and Buddhism. *Psychoanalytic Inquiry*, 28, pp. 541–549.

Index

Notes: Folios followed by "n" refers notes in the text.

Absolute 5, 6, 9n5
adaptational strategies 31
adaptive spiritually sensitive psychoanalytic approach 57–60
Akhtar, S. 43
Alexander, F. 19
Altman, N. 55
analytic experience 46, 87–88
analytic relationship 54, 91–109
area of faith 43–56
Arnold, J. 19
Arnowitz, Y. 2
An Autobiographical Study (Freud) 17, 24

Baal Shem Tov 74n2
Bakan, D. 90n5
Balint, M. 21
Barnett, A.J. 86
Bass, A. 53
Bell, D. 73
Benjamin, J. 31
Berke, J.H. 43, 62–63

Binswanger, L. 17
Bion, W.R. 21, 45, 52–53, 71, 73, 82, 83, 85, 86, 113
Black, D.M. 18
Blass, R. 113, 115
Bohm, D. 53
Bollas, C. 85
Bonaparte, M. 96
Breuer, J. 64
Buddha 65, 87, 91, 120
Buddhism 18, 65–65, 74n1, 79, 89n2, 122

Campbell, F. 21
Caplan, M. 59
Carrington, H. 15
Celenza, A. 95
Civilization and its Discontents (Freud) 14
Cohen, L. 92
Cohen, M. 112
Coltart, N. 44, 62, 121
conscience 36, 63
Cooper, P. 86
Copernican revolution 2

countertransference 32, 46, 96, 98, 100, 107, 115
Crane, J. 19
Cushman, P. 31

Dan, J. 70
De Mello Franco, O.F. 58
De Mornay, R. 92
De Wit, H.F. 118
Dogen, E. 66, 89n2
dream-like event (DLE) 48, 51, 53
Dreher, A.U. 115
Durkheim, E. 23n2
Dworkin, R.: *Religion without God* 36

Ego Psychology 27, 34
Eigen, M. 43–45, 46, 47, 59, 62, 72, 74n4, 79, 84, 87, 117, 120, 121, 122
Einstein, A. 9n4, 107
Eissler, K.R. 28, 90
Enlightenment 23n2, 86, 87
enlightenment practices 122, 123n3
epistemological principle 6
Epstein, M. 65, 89n2
Erikson, E.H.: *Gandhi's truth: On the origins of militant non violence* 20; *Young man Luther: A study in psychoanalysis and history* 20
Esman, A.H. 23n1
The Essence of Christianity (Feuerbach) 23n2
Etezady, M.H. 39
Exclusive Humanism 27

Fairbairn, W.R.D. 20, 32, 97
faith 36–39, 44, 47; Freud's relation to 18; psychoanalysis and 21; religious 13, 15, 18–19; and spirit 20; and spirituality 112
Fauteux, K. 69
Fenichel, O. 18
Ferenczi, S. 32, 33, 97
Feuerbach, L.: *The Essence of Christianity* 23n2
Fink, B. 97
Forman, R.K.C. 5, 6, 35, 71
Fosshage, J.L. 94
Freud, S. 1, 23n2, 34, 46, 63, 64, 77, 78, 85, 88, 96, 109, 111, 119; analytic psychology 28; atheist 20; attack on religion 37; *An Autobiographical Study* 17, 24; Buddhist meditation 90n5; *Civilization and its Discontents* 14; commitment of 26; *The Future of an Illusion* 17–18; *The Interpretation of Dreams* 48; on occultism 16; origins of religiosity in infancy 23n1; on possibility of telepathy 15; primary narcissism 21; on psychoanalysis 123n2; psychoanalytic system 27; *The Psychopathology of Everyday Life* 13; *The Question of a Weltanschauung:* "[A] *Weltanschauung* 25; reductionist theory 71; relation to faith 18; on

religion 14–15; on tenacity of religion 14
Fromm, E. 20, 40n1, 45, 64, 69, 110n3, 118; on analytic therapy 94; *x* experience 71
The Future of an Illusion (Freud) 17–18

Gandhi's truth: On the origins of militant non violence (Erikson) 20
Gargiulo, G.J. 79, 81
Gellner, E. 78
Genoud, C. 87
Gerrard, J. 95, 98, 101, 109
Ghent, E. 68, 69
Giddens, A. 29
Gordon, K. 45, 114
Govrin, A. 31, 44, 46, 117, 120
Green, A. 94
Greifinger, J. 115
Grotstein, J.S. 43, 45, 72

Hadar, U. 62
Hale, N.G. 31
Hartmann, H. 27, 28
Heelas, P. 5
Heraclitus 120
holism 5
Humanism 26–27
Hutcheon, L.: *The Politics of Postmodernity* 34
Huxley, A. 6

incarnating goodness 62
incommunicado element 21, 46
institutional religion 36
The Interpretation of Dreams (Freud) 48

James, W. 36
Jones, E. 16
Jūgyū (Ten Bulls) 88
Jung, C.G. 22, 47, 51, 95; analytical psychology 22
Jungian analytical psychology 47–48
Jurist, E.L. 34

Kant, I. 70, 71
Kenosis 67
Khan, M. 93
Klein, M. 18
Kohut, H. 20, 62, 63, 66
Kubie, L.S. 90
Kurtz, S. 82, 90n4

Lacan, J. 74n1
LaMothe, R. 19, 44
Langan, R. 85
Lawner, P. 84
Leibniz, G.W. 6
Lerner, M. 6
liberation 29, 52, 61, 79, 87, 95, 119
Library of Congress 1
Loewald, H. 20, 103
love 91–109; of analyst for patient 96–109; curative 95

Magid, B. 66, 84
Maharaj, N. 82, 83
Malone, T. 98
Marcus, P. 43, 45, 73
masochism 68
mass-delusions 13
Masters, R. 59
materialist project 45
Meissner, W.W. 44, 47, 118
Meltzer, D. 25
Menninger, K. 94
Merkur, D. 71

meta-narratives 30
Milner, M. 21
Mitchell, S.A. 33, 85
Modell, A.H. 93, 104
Moncayo, R. 74n1
Moore, T. 68–69
morality 61–73
mystical experience 67, 70–73, 79–80, 88, 107, 112, 117
mysticism 20, 21, 70, 79, 118
mystic tradition 52

narcissism 64–65, 91
Neo-Nietzschean perspective 26, 29
Nes, B. 46
New Introductory Lectures (Freud) 15
New Spirituality 37
the numinous 70

occultism 16
oceanic feeling 14, 15
"one person" approach 27, 32, 62, 79, 97
ontological principle 5
O 53, 71–72
O-resistances 73
Otto, R. 70

panentheism 5, 9n3
panentheistic 5, 6
paradigm shift 2, 69, 111
Parsons, W.B. 111
Patañjali: *Yoga Sutras* 78
Perennial Philosophy 5–6
Pfister, O. 18
Phillips, A. 121
Plato 7
The Politics of Postmodernity (Hutcheon) 34
post-modernism 26, 29

post-modernity 31
projective identification 46
Psyche and Soul book series 2
psychoanalysis, cultural history of 24–40; defined 25, 28; influenced by 25; Relational paradigm 33; stress for change in 38; as spiritual practice 77–89
psychoanalytic approach 40n2
psychoanalytic developmental theory 47
psychoanalytic schools 44
psychoanalytic technique 82
psychoanalytic theory 67
psychoneurosis 73
The Psychopathology of Everyday Life (Freud) 13
"Pure Consciousness Events" 71

The Question of a Weltanschauung (Freud) 25

Rangell, L. 116
relational turn 96
religion 34; essence of 35; spirituality and 36
Religion without God (Dworkin) 36
religious instinct 45
Rizzuto, A. M. 43, 44, 58, 79
Roland, A. 43
Rolland, R. 14, 71
Rubin, J.B. 38, 47, 58, 59, 63, 68, 118
Russell, B. 70
Rustin, M. 29

sacred unconscious 47
Samuels, A. 4, 38, 58, 123n1
Sandler, J. 115

Sass, L.A. 31
Schneider, S. 43, 62–63
Searles, H. 98
seductiveness of analytic situation 95
Segal, H. 97
self-emptying *(Kenosis)* 67
self-lessness 61, 73, 116–117
Sen-Gupta, O. 78
Shaw, D. 96, 100, 101, 104
Silberstein, E. 23n1
Simmonds, J.G. 19, 83, 111
Smith, J.H. 61
social unconscious 47
Sorenson, R.L. 1, 40n2, 44, 111
Soul *(die Seele)* 46
soul-centred practices 61
Spero, M.H. 2, 60
spirituality: defined 3, 4; and faith 112; religion and 36
spiritual-turn 44, 74n1
state of surrender 67
Steiner, G. 78, 89n1
Stone, C. 43, 62
Strachey, J. 46
Suzuki, S. 86, 87
Symington, N. 43–44, 63, 64, 81, 92

Tacey, D. 35
Tarnus, R. 25
Taylor, C. 7, 26, 30, 34

Tennes, M. 46, 53, 54
Teresa of Ávila 88
Thorne, B. 97
total composite analytic theory 116
Totton, N. 122
transcendence 61–73
transference 46
true religiosity 9n4

Ulanov, A.B. 7
unio mystica 21

Vyasa 78

Wallerstein, R.S. 27, 28, 85, 117
Weltanschauung 24–28, 33, 36–39, 44, 111
Winnicott, D.W. 21, 46, 55–56, 66, 93, 103
Wittgenstein, L. 70
worldview, defined 25

x experience 20, 69, 71

Yoga Sutras (Patañjali) 78
Young-Eisendrath, P. 89n2
Young man Luther: A study in psychoanalysis and history (Erikson) 20

Zen Buddhism 2, 20, 66, 69, 82, 84, 86, 88, 104, 121